CELEBRATION OF
AMERICAN
LIFE

BARB ADAMS

ALMA ALLEN

Appliqué patterns honoring a nation and its people

Kansas City Star Books, 2002

CELEBRATION
OF
AMERICAN LIFE

BARB ADAMS
&
ALMA ALLEN

Celebration of American Life
Appliqué Patterns Honoring A Nation
and Its People
By Barb Adams and Alma Allen
History introduction and profiles by
Jane Fifield Flynn
Edited by Doug Weaver and Sue Spade
Book design by Sue Spade
Photography by Bill Krzyzanowski
Production assistance by Jo Ann Groves
Graphics by Gentry Mullen, Sue Spade
and Sara Livingston
Portraits by Sue Spade

Published by Kansas City Star Books
1729 Grand Blvd., Kansas City, Missouri ,
64108
All rights reserved.
Copyright © 2002 by The Kansas City
Star Co.

First Edition, first printing
Library of Congress Control Number:
2002111484
ISBN:0-9722739-3-X

Printed in the United States of America
by Walsworth Publishing Co.

To order copies, call StarInfo,
(816-234-4636)

www.PickleDish.com

CONTENTS

AT LEFT: UNITED WE STAND CROSS-STITCH PILLOW ON ALMA'S QUILT

$\mathcal{I}$NTRODUCTION

$\mathcal{T}$he symbolism contained in pattern and fabric has long been the silent voice of women. So it is with quilts.

In "Celebration of American Life," we use some of those symbols to represent the values in life we cherish. Flowers and plants always have carried certain meanings. The olive branch's offering of peace is certainly familiar to many, for example.

Each value, and thus each block, was chosen for the ideal it represents. These are the goals for which we as a nation and people strive.

This book is an outgrowth of a block-of-the-month project that first appeared dur-ing 2002 in *The Kansas City Star's* Sunday magazine, *Star Magazine*. The Star has a long history of printing quilt patterns in its newspaper (the first ones appeared in 1928).

Of course, a book is more than the product of just the authors. We owe much to the following people: Jane Fifield Flynn, author of "Kansas City Women of Independent Minds," has written the biog-raphies that accompany the patterns in this book. Her stories of everyday women in our community who exemplify these values add greatly to our appreciation of both women's history and the power of the individual.

Sue Spade's wonderful pen and ink

ALMA ALLEN, LEFT, AND BARB ADAMS

drawings bring these women to life. Her artwork adds to our perception of the theme. Her watercolor brush vividly depicts our nation's spacious skies. And, of course, her compelling and beautiful design of this book is the glue that holds it together.

Bill Kryzyanowski, our photographer, is an essential part of our team. He inspires us and brings our designs to life.

Gentry Mullen's skilled work in computer graphics made the patterns accurate and easy to understand.

The following women also need to be recognized for their long hours and tremendous skills: Jean Stanclift and Leona Adams assisted with the appliqué of our blocks; Jeane Zyck and Sharyn Rigg quilted the tops; Joy Hayward and Sylvia Webb stitched our cross-stitch sampler and pillow; Sara Livingston graphed the cross-stitch designs for the book.

Also, C.C. & Company provided the frame for the sampler; Minerva Cabanas hooked our rug; Marilyn Schmidt overdyed the wool for the rug; Kathleen Johnson stitched the pincushion; Leona Adams designed and crocheted the flag pillow and stitched the blue-work pillow.

And many thanks to our editor, Doug Weaver of Kansas City Star Books, for giving us the opportunity to do this project. His experience and calm guidance are greatly appreciated.

Finally, thanks to you quilters for allowing us to share our vision with you. We hope that you, too, will celebrate your life as an American through these patterns.

— BARB ADAMS AND ALMA ALLEN,
KANSAS CITY, MO., SEPTEMBER 2002

ℋer Story

Jane Fifield Flynn

𝒜ny time is a good time to celebrate the attributes that make American life great. But the tragic events of recent months lend considerable poignancy to that discussion today.

For quilters, it's also an appropriate time to reflect on the role of American women in our history – pioneer women who traversed the plains; city women who led their communities by example; women who today sacrifice much as they serve in the armed forces.

The Celebration of American Life quilt project was launched by Barb Adams and Alma Allen as a way to honor both the sinew that binds us together as Americans and the role of women in this American life.

That I should be part of this project is, to me, somewhat a surprise. I know little about quilting. But I do know about

women who became leaders at a time when their leadership was not necessarily welcome.

In my book, "Kansas City Women of Independent Minds," I identified dozens of women who helped profoundly shape a young community. So it was relatively easy to match Barb and Alma's quilt blocks with women who illustrated each block's virtue.

Don't assume, though, that these women came by these associations easily. For the most part these women were heroes, yet they were obscured for decades by societal indifference. The roles assigned to women before the turn of the century were very constricted, conventional and a reflection of the Victorian mode of behavior. Risk-taking was left to men, and women who revealed an interest in or knowledge of issues beyond those of one's own house-

SEEKING THE RIGHT TO VOTE, SUFFRAGISTS FROM THROUGHOUT MISSOURI GATHERED IN JEFFERSON CITY TO LOBBY STATE LAWMAKERS IN THE MID-1910s.

hold were forbidden.

However, there began to emerge a few women who sought in subtle ways to create for themselves and others a more meaningful life.

In Kansas City the seed was sown in February 1881 when Sarah Chandler Coates invited a few of her friends to join her at home for a luncheon. Not intended as a social gathering, it was to explore a radical idea. Coates suggested forming a women's group for the express purpose of discussing literature.

Wary of how their husbands would react, the women decided to forego calling the group a club but to refer to the activity as a class. From a few, the class grew. It was obvious that many women were intellectually starving. Coates, when asked later about her motivation in forming the club, responded, "To stimulate torpid minds." Other clubs formed to study subjects such as Shakespeare's writings, art, music and current events.

DRESSED FOR MOTORING: THEIR CAR IS A HALLADY, THEIR DEALER BERGERS AUTOMOBILE CO.

Building on a new sense of confidence, these insurgents began to look out into the

community and observed that much was needed to make it a healthier and more equitable city. Men, they noted, everlastingly dwelt within political party lines, arguing over elected offices and ward boundaries but accomplishing little. A few lessons in accomplishments were needed!

And the women responded. Aware that the city council and property owners had spent considerable time and energy formulating a plan to equip playgrounds in the city's north end, a group of women stepped in and finally got the job done. The county courts had for years been unable to agree on a solution to improve the deplorable conditions at the county farm. Appalled by what they saw, a number of women took the court to task resulting in the construction

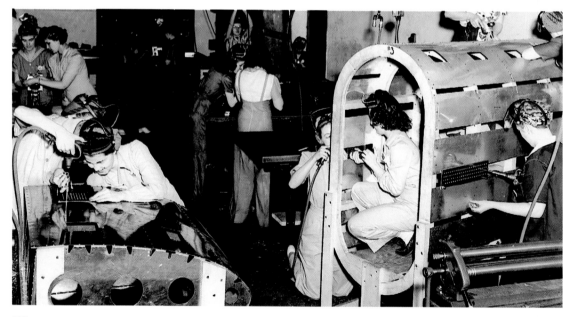

WITH THOUSANDS OF MEN OFF TO WAR, WOMEN ENTERED THE WORK FORCE.

of a new home.

The list of goals became long: Better housing, better health care for the indigent, improved sanitation, development of musical opportunities as well as of literature.

Soon Coates took on her next cause — the right of women to vote.

Although Coates would die before her crusade was finished, Phebe Rout Ess took on the cause. She formed and was elected the first president of the Kansas City Equal Suffrage Association, gaining national recognition as a champion of equal rights. The right of women to vote was far from popular with most men, and many women supporters were at times in physical jeopardy. More often, they were publicly humiliated.

So many others did so much to help improve the American human condition, bringing comfort and hope for a better life. Della Cochran Lamb opened a day nursery for working mothers. Angie Aker sought to improve the quality of life for sufferers of sicle cell anemia by educating blacks on the importance of blood tests to identify carriers. Claude Gorton faced head-on the Pendergast political machine by motivating women to work in politics and aid in cleaning out City Hall. Sophia Rosenberger, a teacher, possessed remarkable abilities to inspire and instill in students the joy of reading. Leona Pouncy Thurman, the first black woman to practice law in Kansas City,

FEMALE ARMY AIR CORP CADETS TOOK STANCES IN THE GREAT WAR.

was one of the most avid champions of revitalization of the 18th & Vine jazz area.

Those acknowledged above represent such a small number of the deserving — of those who broke with tradition to be the first women in a field or persevered in a non-traditional female profession.

In the following pages, you'll learn of other women who achieved much in their time. How appropriate that the 12 women identified here coincide with 12 quilt blocks that, stitched together, make a defining statement about our American Life.

To such women, known and unknown, we all owe a huge debt of gratitude.

PRELUDE

*Here, then, are the 12 blocks that make up the
Celebration of American Life quilt. Each block
presentation includes a detailed photograph of the
block, the profile of a Kansas City woman who
inspired the theme, and a template.*

*History profiles were contributed by Jane Fiefield
Flynn, author of "Kansas City Women of
Independent Minds."*

Basic Appliqué Instructions

■ Cut 12 squares 18-1/2" x 18-1/2" from
the background fabrics. This measurement includes a 1/4" seam allowance.

■ Use freezer paper to make templates of
the appliqué shapes.

■ Cut the paper shapes out. Do not add a
seam allowance to the paper shapes.

■ Iron the slick side of the paper shapes to
the right side of your fabric. Use a mark-
ing pencil that will show up on your fabric and trace around the shape for needle turn appliqué. The drawn line indi-
cates your seam line.

■ Cut the fabric shapes out, now adding
your seam allowance.

■ Fold the background fabric in half verti-
cally and horizontally. Finger-press the
folds. Open the fabric. These fold lines
will assist you in centering your design
on the background block.

■ Place the shapes on your piece of background fabric.

ABOVE: BARB'S QUILT
WITH THE BLUE WORK
PILLOW. LEFT: DETAIL OF
BARB'S QUILT.

■ Remove the freezer paper.

■ Baste shapes into place on the background block.

■ Appliqué the shapes to the background.

Block ONE

PATRIOTISM

Our inspiration:

KATHARINE LEE
BATES *(1859-1929)*

$\mathcal{B}$ATES, AN ENGLISH LITERATURE PROFESSOR at Wellesley College, gave us "America, America," a poem that became the patriotic song "America the Beautiful."

In the summer of 1893, Bates made her first trip West by train to teach summer classes in Colorado. On July 4, the train reached the Kansas prairie, where wheat and prairie grasses waved in the summer wind. The vast expanse of Kansas made a strong impression on Bates. It made her "a better American," as she wrote in her journal that day.

The next day Bates arrived in Colorado Springs for her summer teaching session. In her spare time she explored the area, sightseeing.

The "supreme day of our Colorado sojourn" came near the end of her visit. The teachers were invited to travel to the top of Pikes Peak. The view during her brief visit moved her.

"It was then and there," she wrote, "as I was looking out over the sealike expanse of fertile country spreading away so far under those ample skies, that the opening lines of the hymn floated into my mind."

Oh beautiful for spacious skies,
For amber waves of grain,
For purple mountain majesties
Above the fruited plain!
America! America!
God shed his grace on thee
And crown thy good with brotherhood
From sea to shining sea.

To learn more about Katharine Lee Bates, check out the book "America the Beautiful" by Lynn Sherr (Public Affairs, 2001).

Completed block

Patriotism Block Symbolism:

Our flag is a popular symbol in Americana folk art. The flag, with its red, white and blue, symbolizes the love we feel for our country. The flower is the lily. The lily represents majesty – the majesty of our skies and the land we hold dear. The vine of honeysuckle represents the devotion to our country's values.

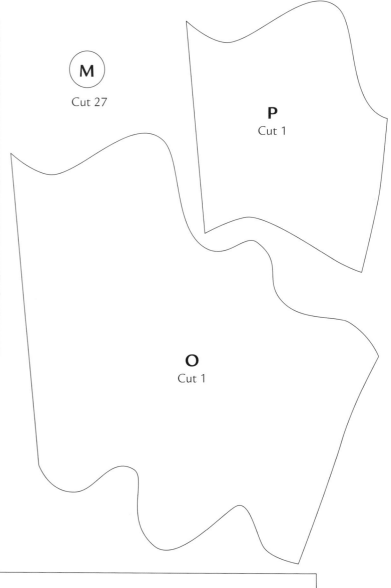

Pattern represents 1/2 of block at 39%

18

Block TWO

Our inspiration:

ANGIE SANDIFER AKER *(1911-1990)*

*I*F THE ACCUMULATION OF MONEY is used to judge one's worth, Angie Sandifer Aker would surely be counted among the worthless. She came into this world with nary two nickels to rub together and left with little more.

But if wealth is measured by caring and compassion, Aker ranks as a multimillionaire.

Born one of nine children of Mississippi sharecroppers, she managed only an eighth-grade education, and even that came at a price. White children would pass her in covered wagons as she walked to school, taunting her and spitting on her.

But what could have been a devastating childhood was countered by strength within her family, and especially from her mother, who taught her right from wrong.

Aker arrived with six children in Kansas City in 1943. A short time later, she became a widow and took on menial jobs to support the family. But then another blow befell her. Two of her sons were diagnosed with sickle cell anemia. Both died, one at 16, the other at 26.

From this tragedy, Angie found her mission in life. She founded the Kansas City Chapter of Sickle Cell Inc. Because she understood the debilitation of the disease, she was on call day and night to offer comfort.

Angie also cast an eye on the plight of the elderly, particularly those of lower income. She was one of the founders of a central-city chapter of the American Association of Retired Persons.

In 1975 she was named Woman of the Year of a seven-state area by AARP. A year later, she was honored by President Gerald Ford as an International Woman of the Year.

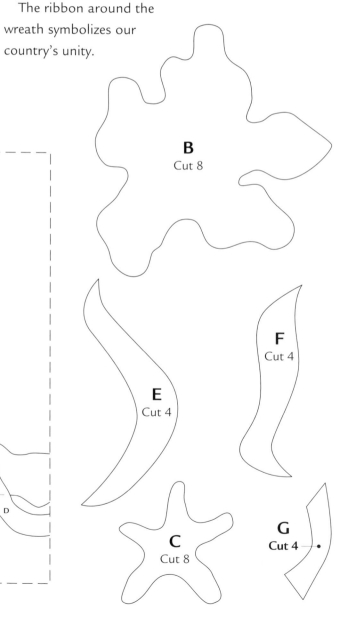

Diversity Block Symbolism:

The elements in the Diversity block were chosen to reflect our country's diverse ideas, beliefs and population. The poppy flower represents the wonder of our dreams for the future. Adams and Allen chose it to illustrate Martin Luther King Jr.'s inspirational "I Have a Dream" speech.

The willow wreath is symbolic for its healing properties. The willow is found worldwide and able to grow in varying climates. It represents citizens from throughout the world, who put down roots and spread their branches to establish homes, families and businesses in America.

The ribbon around the wreath symbolizes our country's unity.

Completed block

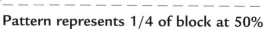

Pattern represents 1/4 of block at 50%

22

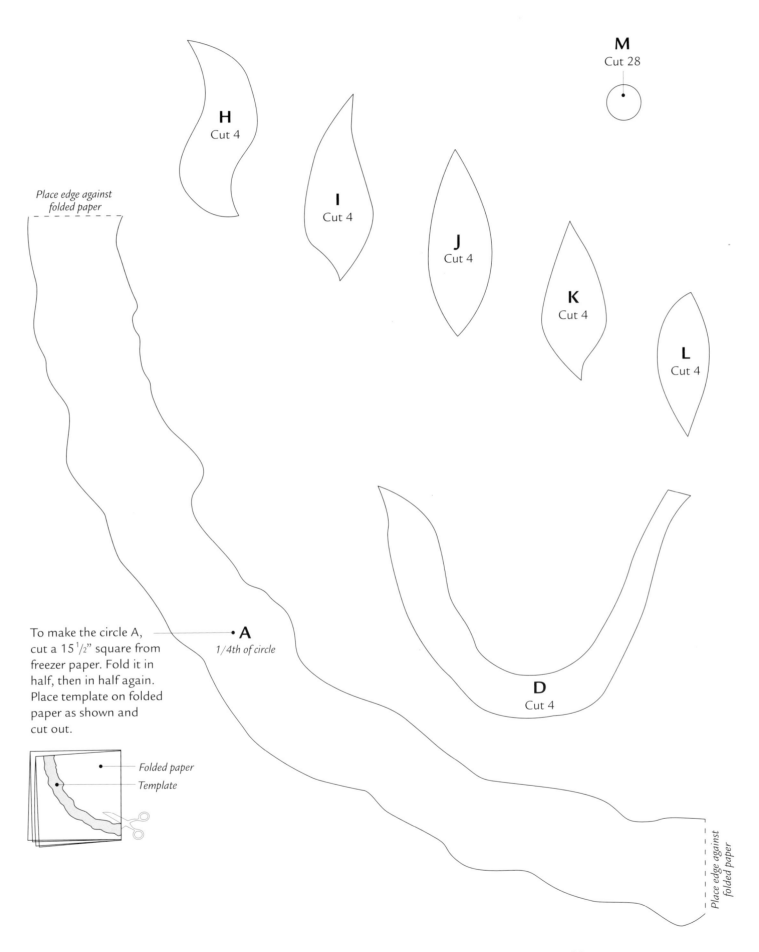

M
Cut 28

H
Cut 4

I
Cut 4

J
Cut 4

K
Cut 4

L
Cut 4

Place edge against folded paper

•**A**
1/4th of circle

To make the circle A, cut a 15¹/₂" square from freezer paper. Fold it in half, then in half again. Place template on folded paper as shown and cut out.

Folded paper
Template

D
Cut 4

Place edge against folded paper

Block THREE

OPPORTUNITY

Our inspiration:

ANNIE J. SCOTT

*I*N TURN-OF-THE-CENTURY KANSAS CITY, no woman better exemplified a rags-to-riches rise in a man's world than Annie J. Scott.

As a penniless orphan, she was sent to live on a farm in Lafayette County, Mo. Working from dawn to dusk, she performed all the menial duties a family of 10 required.

But it was a chance encounter that started her climb up the ladder of not one profession but several. Visitors to the farm spoke of a town named Warrensburg and a school there, the Warrensburg Normal School.

Scott saved every penny she earned. At 14, with $50 and her few belongings tied in a bundle, she enrolled at Warrensburg. Three years later, she graduated with a teaching certificate.

Scott then decided to pursue Methodist missionary work. Entering the Scarritt Bible and Methodist Training School in Kansas City, she was offered the job of state secretary of the Epworth League. But the traveling and teaching were so physically demanding that she suffered a collapse severe enough to require hospitalization.

While recovering she wrote several children's Bible books. But she also grew fascinated with medicine, which led her to the Medical College of the University of Kansas, where she eventually graduated third in her class of mostly male students.

Turn-of-the-century female physicians were not welcome into private practices, but Scott was fortunate. The city was in the throes of a smallpox epidemic, so she was hired immediately. She also managed to save $2,000 from her meager salary.

A colleague, along with another partner, suggested she invest the money in the purchase of 11 acres along State Line Road between 43rd and 45th streets. Selling the property in small lots, Scott became her own real estate agent, architect, contractor and builder. Between 1904 and 1909, she supervised the construction of more than 200 houses.

Her achievements make her KC's foremost self-made woman.

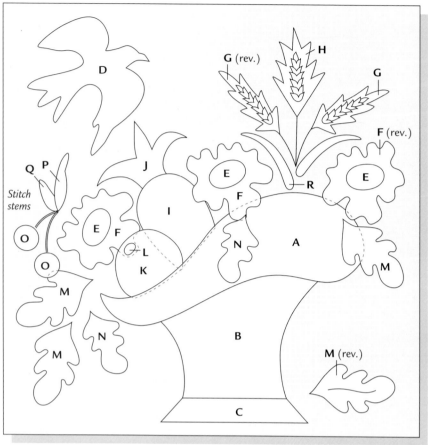

Completed block

Opportunity Block Symbolism:

In this block, the basket, representing our country, contains an abundance of symbols. The flower is a red chrysanthemum representing hope. The pineapple represents our hospitality, as we welcome ideas and plans for the future. The orange symbolizes prosperity; the grain, productivity. The cherries represent the good education we all wish for our children.

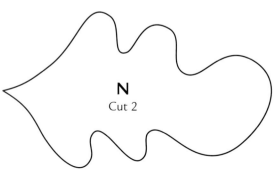

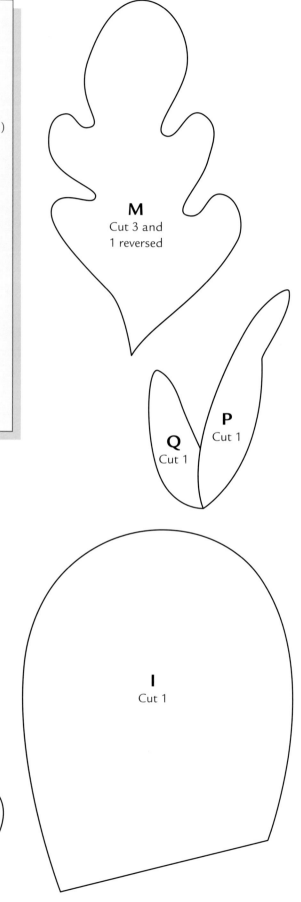

O
Cut 2

D
Cut 1

R
Cut 1 and
1 reversed

1 3 5 7
2 4 6 8

*Stem stitch for cherry
and leaf stems.*

Note: *Use DMC floss
in contrasting color for
stem stitch detail. Use
four strands of floss.*

L
Cut 1

K
Cut 1

E
Cut 3

F
Cut 2 and
1 reversed

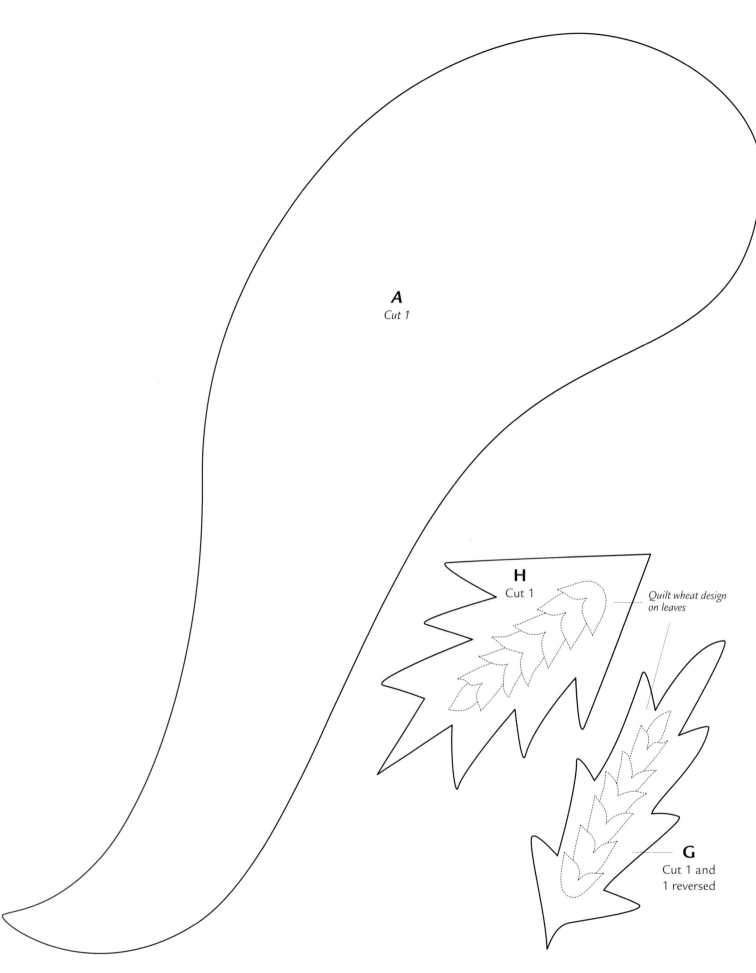

A
Cut 1

H
Cut 1

*Quilt wheat design
on leaves*

G
Cut 1 and
1 reversed

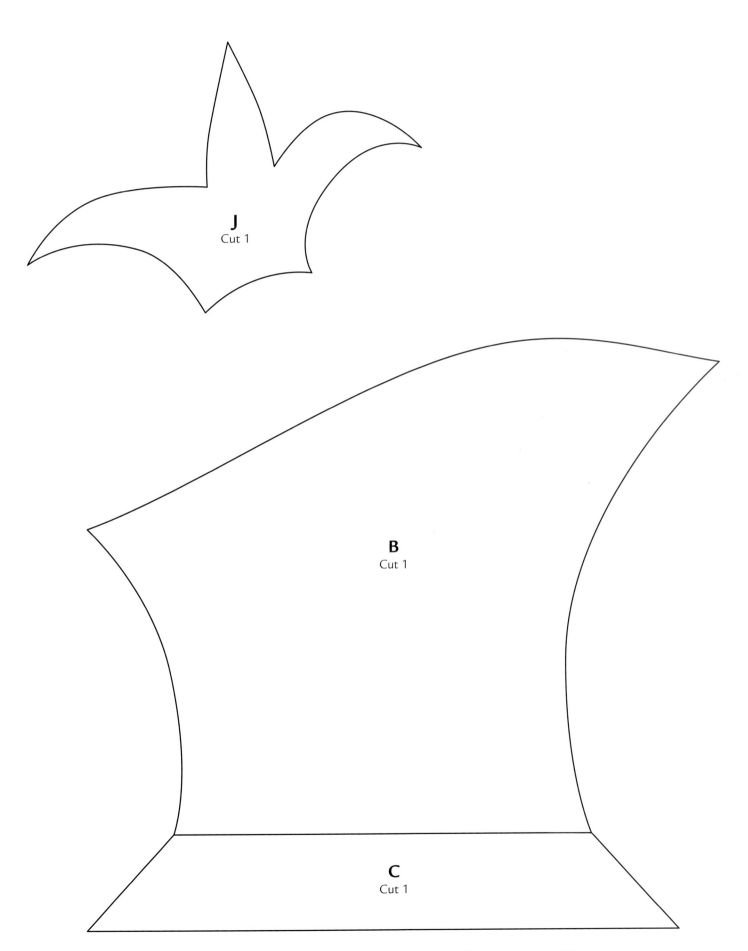

J
Cut 1

B
Cut 1

C
Cut 1

Block FOUR

COMMUNITY

Our inspiration:

MINNIE LEE
CROSTHWAITE *(1872-1963)*

$\mathcal{M}$INNIE LEE CROSTHWAITE, one of Kansas City's first black social workers, touched the lives of many as a community fund-raiser, education advocate and leader.

She was born in Nashville in 1872. After completing public school, she entered Fisk University, where she received a teaching degree. The teaching career didn't last long, though, ending when she moved to Kansas City with her husband, Dr. David N. Crosthwaite.

After her three children were old enough to not require her full attention, Crosthwaite volunteered with the Provident Hospital Association. It took her only a short time to realize there was a great need for trained social workers in the black community. To learn those skills, she enrolled in a nine-week course at the New York School of Social Welfare. Returning to Kansas City in 1922, she became a full-time social worker with what had become Wheatley-Provident Hospital. Several years later, she was named the director of the hospital's outpatient clinic.

To raise funds for critically needed hospital equ initiated a benefit fashion show that became an ani Municipal Auditorium. Her efforts raised enough fi hospital's mortgage, buy a new X-ray machine kitchen, and purchase and remodel a home for t nurses.

Her efforts were not limited to just the hospital was one of the first members of the Woman's Leag instrumental in getting manual training introduce schools. She also served as city and state president Association of Colored Women, and was also a American Association of Social Workers, the NAAC YWCA.

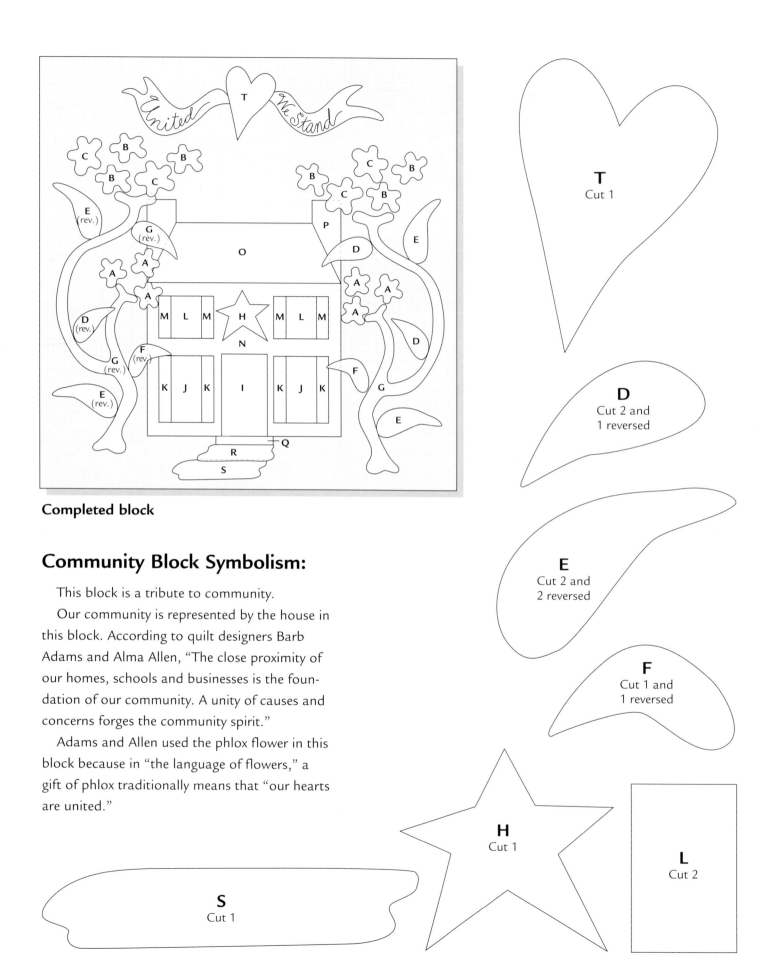

Completed block

Community Block Symbolism:

This block is a tribute to community.

Our community is represented by the house in this block. According to quilt designers Barb Adams and Alma Allen, "The close proximity of our homes, schools and businesses is the foundation of our community. A unity of causes and concerns forges the community spirit."

Adams and Allen used the phlox flower in this block because in "the language of flowers," a gift of phlox traditionally means that "our hearts are united."

T
Cut 1

D
Cut 2 and
1 reversed

E
Cut 2 and
2 reversed

F
Cut 1 and
1 reversed

H
Cut 1

L
Cut 2

S
Cut 1

V
Cut 1

U
Cut 1

1 3 5 7
2 4 6 8

Stem stitch for "United We Stand" script

Note: *Use contrasting DMC floss for the lettering. Use three strands of floss when stitching the lettering.*

G
Cut 1 and
1 reversed

A
Cut 6

C
Cut 4

B
Cut 6

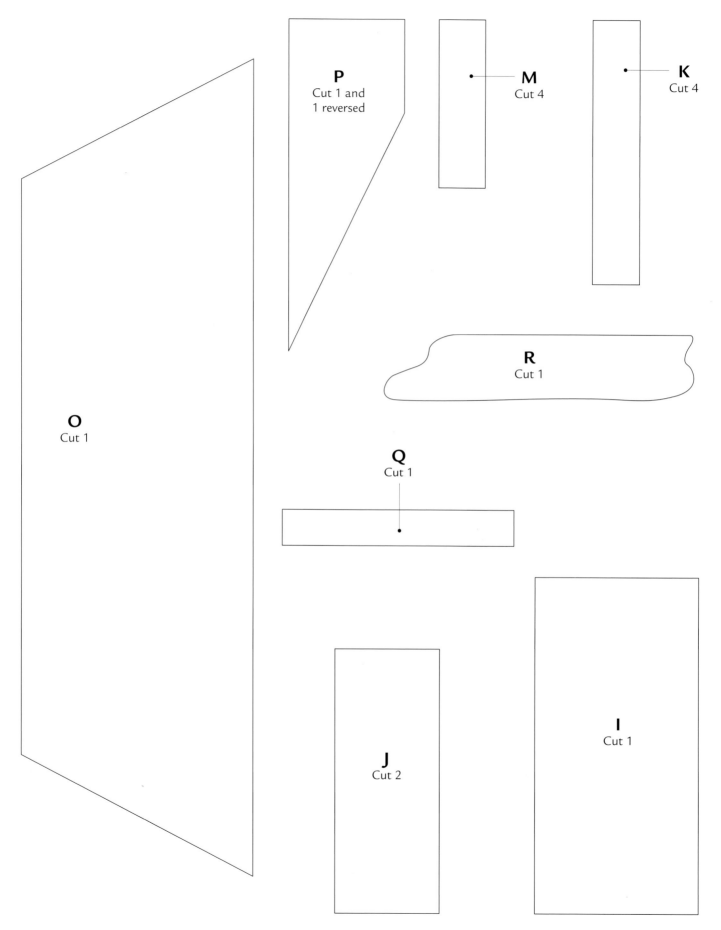

P
Cut 1 and
1 reversed

M
Cut 4

K
Cut 4

R
Cut 1

O
Cut 1

Q
Cut 1

I
Cut 1

J
Cut 2

N
Cut 1

Block FIVE

REMEMBRANCE

Our inspiration:

MAE REED
PORTER *(1888-1968)*

$\mathcal{I}$T WAS THE "MIGHTY MO," the Missouri River flowing past her home in Glascow, Mo., that fueled her childhood imagination. And that in turn led to Mae Reed's lifelong passion for the history of the American West. Her inspiration included the Lewis and Clark expedition, the paddlewheels heading up river loaded with cargo of supplies and passengers, and of the venturesome seeking their fortunes.

Mae Reed met Clyde Henderson Porter while they were both attending Iowa State College. They married in 1910, eventually moving to Kansas City where her husband joined his father at the Kansas City Power and Light Co.

Porter gained respect as a noted author, lecturer and world traveler, building a reputation as a serious and knowledgeable collector of American Indian relics. It was in 1937, however, when fate placed in her hands a treasure trove.

She and her daughter were visiting the Peale Museum in Baltimore when she discovered a collection of sketches by Alfred Jacob Miller done in 1837 and 1838 during a hunting trip with Sir William Drummond Stewart. He was a Scotsman who had come to America to learn about the American Indians. The sketches totaled 300, about 100 of which were found by Porter in a pasteboard box in the museum's attic, where they had been sitting for more than a century. Porter bought the sketches for $800.

She thoroughly researched each of the sketches, which eventually resulted in a slide show accompanied by a lecture. Entitled "The West That Was," it was the first draft of a later work that would prove famous.

That occurred after Porter was introduced to the well-known historian, Bernard DeVeto. He took her draft for a book, selected the sketches, and authored "Across the Wide Missouri," which then won a Pulitzer Prize. Porter was asked to write the forward for the book. A movie version, starring Clark Gable, premiered in Kansas City at the Loew's Midland Theater in 1951.

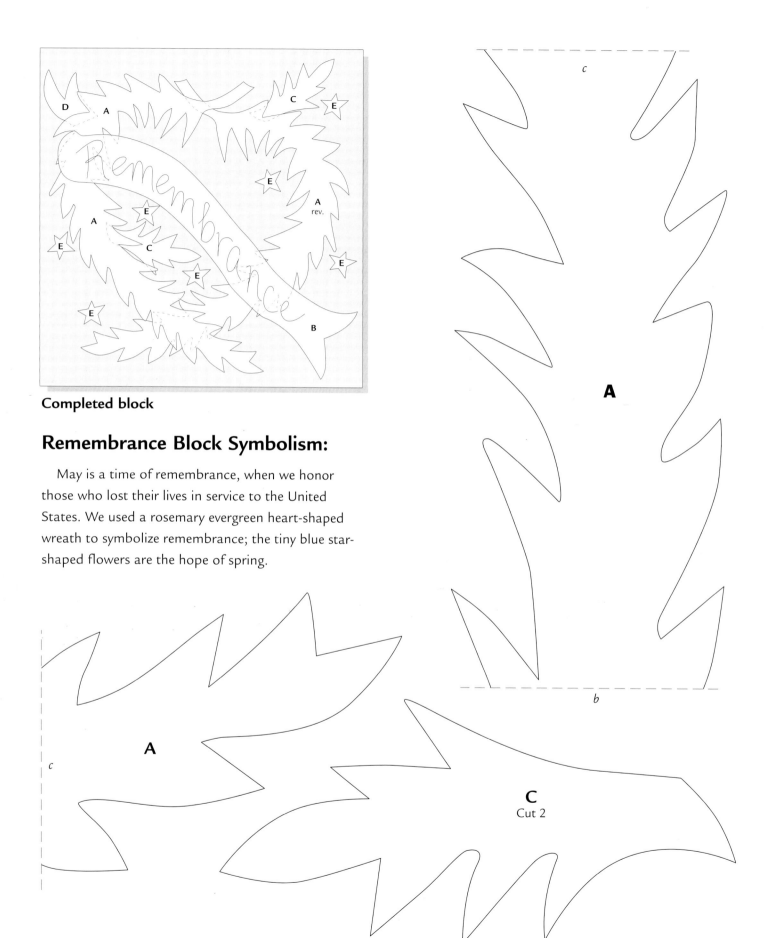

Completed block

Remembrance Block Symbolism:

May is a time of remembrance, when we honor those who lost their lives in service to the United States. We used a rosemary evergreen heart-shaped wreath to symbolize remembrance; the tiny blue star-shaped flowers are the hope of spring.

C
Cut 2

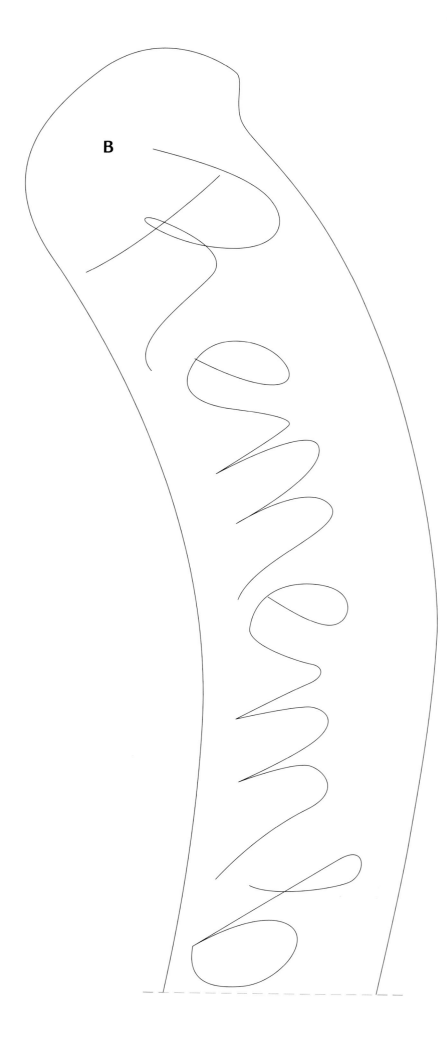

B
Cut 1

To create full-size pattern, cut out
pattern pieces and tape
together as indicated above.

1 3 5 7
2 4 6 8

*Stem stitch for
"Remembrance" script*

Note: *Use DMC floss in contrasting color for stem stitch detail.
Use three strands of floss.*

A
Cut 1 and
1 reversed

To create full-size pattern, cut out
pattern pieces and tape
together as indicated.

D
Cut 1

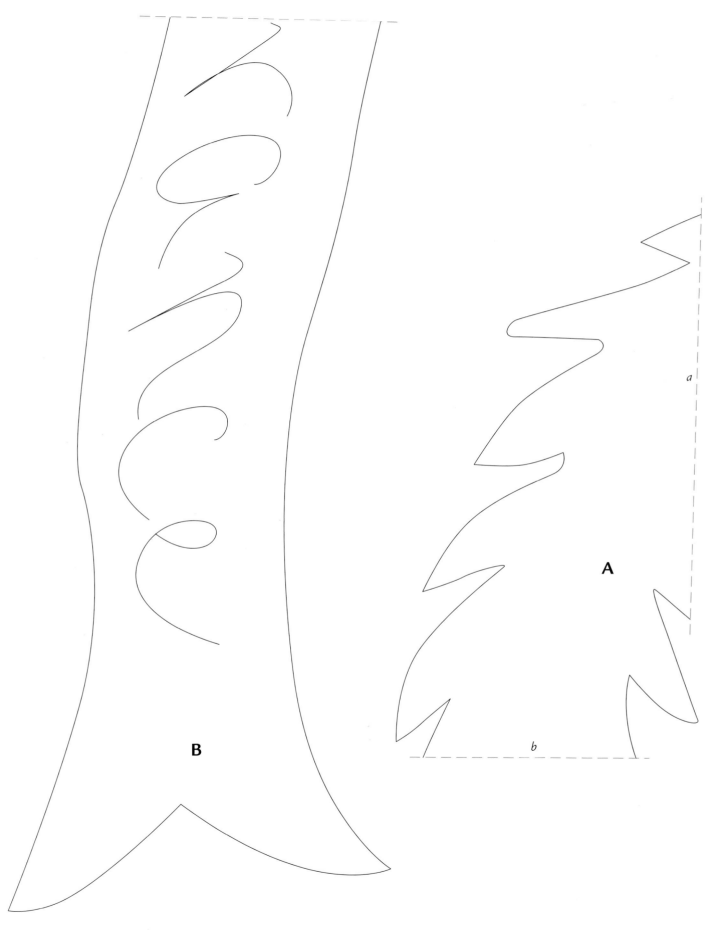

A

B

a

b

40

E
Cut 7

A

a

Block SIX

 *J*USTICE

Our inspiration:

MARY TIERA FARROW (1880-1971)

*H*ER CREDENTIALS AND ACCOMPLISHMENTS were awesome, so much so that she became known as the "Dean of Women Lawyers." No small accomplishment, given that Mary Tiera Farrow pursued a law degree when women were not welcomed into the field.

Farrow was born in Indiana and later moved with her family to Delphos, Kan. Her father opened a general store, which gave her a chance to listen to local lore and stories about Abe Lincoln. She became a deep admirer of Lincoln, leading her to follow his career and enter law.

She came to Kansas City, eventually enrolling in a business school. Then, in 1901, she entered the Kansas City School of Law as the only woman in the class of 80 men.

After gaining her law diploma in 1903, she found a position with a Kansas law firm paying $60 a month. Her skills were noted, and she was elected the city treasurer of Kansas City, Kan., the first female public official in the city.

Farrow then formed a partnership with another law school graduate, Anna L. Donahue, and opened an office in the New York Life Building, handling mainly small cases such as divorces and wills. Although well qualified and experienced, Farrow was blackballed from joining the Kansas City Bar Association.

Regardless, two years later, Farrow was appointed temporary judge of one of the divisions of the Jackson County Circuit Court — the first woman to hold such an appointment.

Farrow's academic accomplishments were considerable, including master's degrees from the University of Illinois and Columbia University. She also did summer work at the Sorbonne and at Oxford University. She was active in the woman's suffrage movement and served in the motor corps during World War I.

To create full-size pattern, cut out
pattern pieces and tape
together as indicated above.

Completed block

Justice Block Symbolism:

The equal placement of the fern fronds
in the Justice block reflects the balance
of what is just or due. The fern
was chosen because it
represents sincerity.

A
Cut 1 and
1 reversed

C
Cut 1

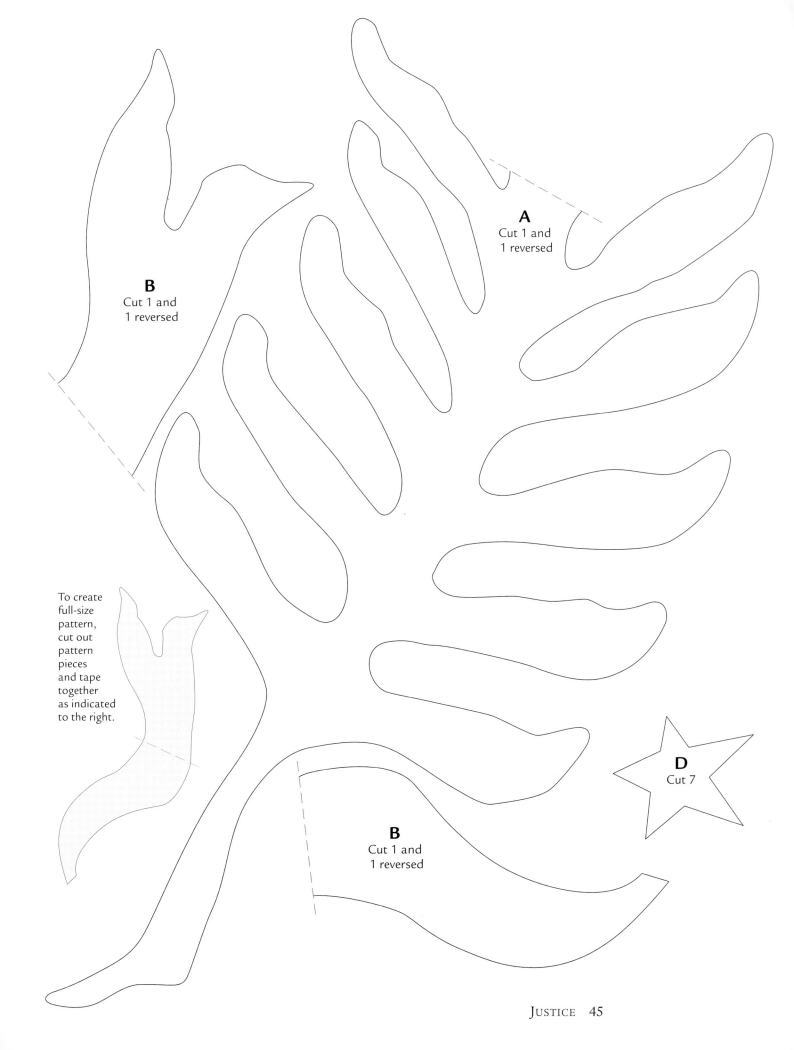

A
Cut 1 and
1 reversed

B
Cut 1 and
1 reversed

To create
full-size
pattern,
cut out
pattern
pieces
and tape
together
as indicated
to the right.

D
Cut 7

B
Cut 1 and
1 reversed

Block SEVEN

$\mathscr{L}$IBERTY

Our inspiration:

ESTHER SWIRK BROWN *(1917-1970)*

*E*STHER SWIRK BROWN DAZZLED HER MANY FRIENDS with her physical beauty. But it was her spiritual pursuit of civil rights and shared liberty that changed the lives of so many.

Born Sept. 17, 1917, in Kansas City, she attended Frances Willard Elementary School and Paseo High School. She studied at the University of Chicago and Northwestern University. Her major was sociology, which provided the foundation for her career as a civil rights crusader.

After she married Paul Brown, the boy who lived across the street, in 1943, she became a typical suburban housewife living in Johnson County. But she was much more than that.

When working for the passage of a school bond issue for the South Park district of Merriam, she discovered appalling conditions in a school for black children. An irate Brown removed the children from the school, arranged a temporary location in homes of families, and taught classes herself. She stated, "I wouldn't want my children to go to a school like that. Why should someone else?"

When she had raised enough money to provide qualified teachers, Brown rolled up her sleeves to right what she regarded as the terrible wrong that had enabled the situation to fester. This time she worked through the courts — and won. In 1949 the Kansas Supreme Court outlawed the system of gerrymandering that deprived black children of equal education facilities and opportunities.

Brown also prodded the National Association for the Advancement of Colored People to pursue the historic Brown vs. Board of Education of Topeka case, in which the Supreme Court ruled that segregated schools deprive minorities of equal educations.

Through her crusading, she touched the lives of thousands. She died on May 24, 1970.

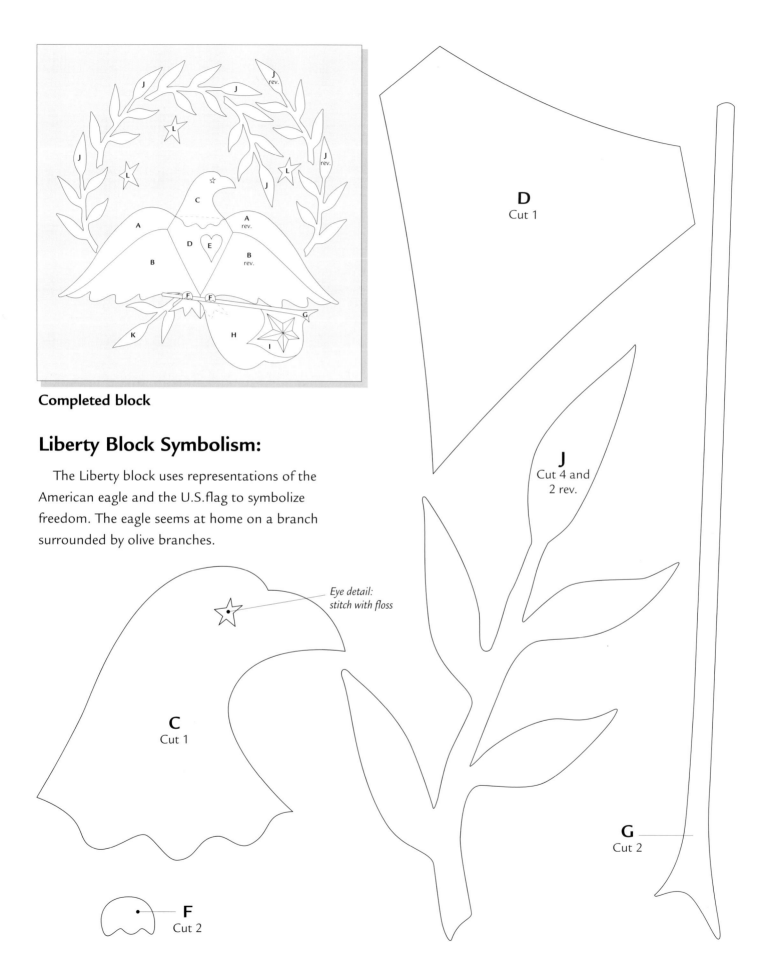

Completed block

Liberty Block Symbolism:

The Liberty block uses representations of the American eagle and the U.S. flag to symbolize freedom. The eagle seems at home on a branch surrounded by olive branches.

D
Cut 1

J
Cut 4 and
2 rev.

*Eye detail:
stitch with floss*

C
Cut 1

G
Cut 2

F
Cut 2

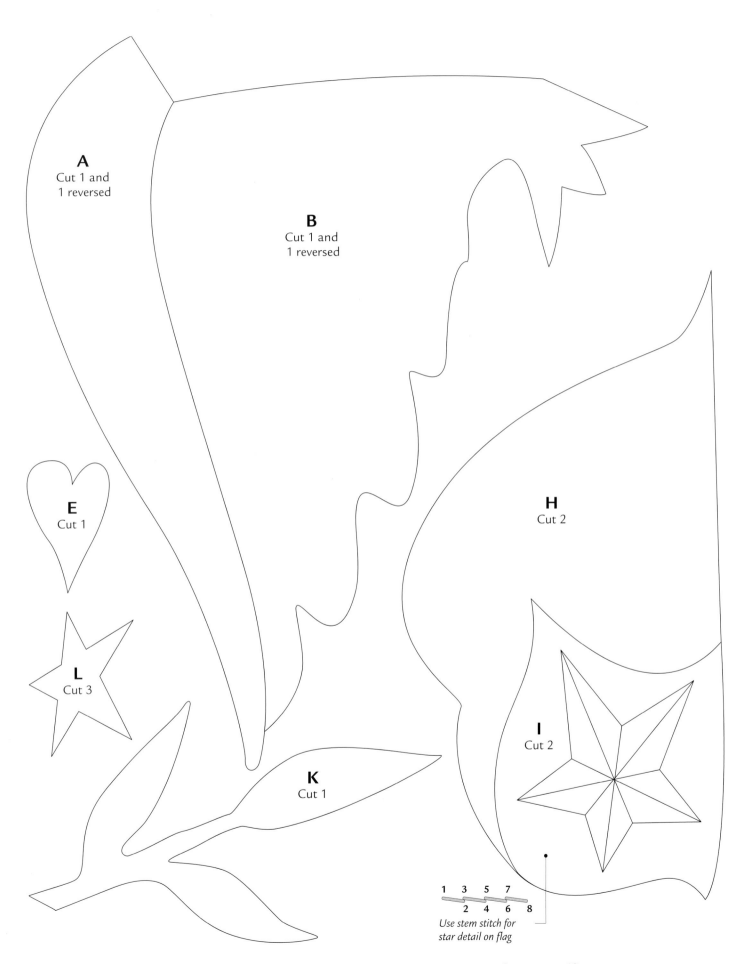

A
Cut 1 and
1 reversed

B
Cut 1 and
1 reversed

E
Cut 1

H
Cut 2

L
Cut 3

K
Cut 1

I
Cut 2

1 3 5 7
2 4 6 8

*Use stem stitch for
star detail on flag*

Block EIGHT

THRIFT

Our inspiration:

MARY McAFEE
ATKINS *(cir.1835-1911)*

*T*HE OFT USED CLICHES, "Waste not, want not," and "a penny saved is a penny earned," can most aptly be used to describe the life practices of Mary McFee Atkins.

Born in about 1835 in Lawrenceburg, Ky., McFee taught school prior to her marriage to James Burris Atkins, a widower of many years. Eventually settling in Kansas City, her husband formed a real estate business partnership with Andrew T. Jenkins. The partnership made shrewd investments in property located in the city's business district and in land in Clay County. Fate would eventually intervene. After only five years of marriage, now Mary McFee Atkins was left a widow — a very wealthy widow.

She assumed financial responsibility for her husband's affairs. She would manage them wisely. Indeed, at the time of her own death, the estate would be valued at more than $1 million. Neither close friends nor acquaintances had the slightest inkling of her wealth.

The frugality practiced during her youth continued in later years. She appeared to be on the cusp of financial distress. In fact, she avoided what she considered unnecessary expenses.

However, a most particular change occurred, a metamorphosis, in fact. With the urging of her niece, Atkins agreed to take a trip to Europe – much to the disbelief of those who knew her. In 1902, she set sail and for seven summers thereafter she repeated the trip, always traveling alone. The beauty of the classics awakened in her a passion for art that had been dormant for more than seven decades. Her most frequently visited sites included The Louvre, Pitte Palace and the National Gallery in London.

Atkins died on Oct. 13, 1911, in Colorado Springs. The disposition of her estate included very generous gifts to friends, relatives and to several churches. A remaining $200,000 was designated to the construction of a museum. This wish was fulfilled with the death of William Rockhill Nelson in 1915 when the Atkins' trustees relinquished their trust to the Nelson trust. The Nelson Gallery-Atkins Museum, considered one of the nation's leading art museums, opened in 1933, due greatly to the thrift of Mary McFee Atkins.

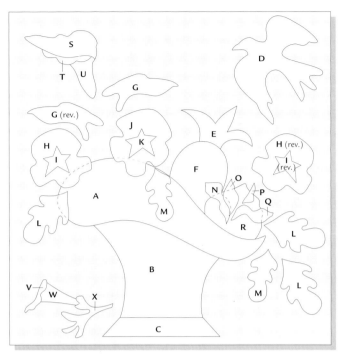

Completed block

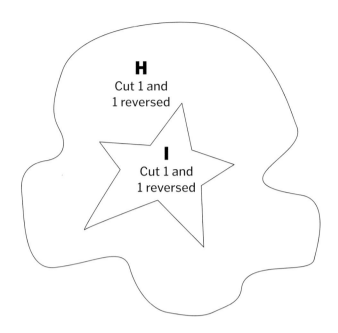

H
Cut 1 and
1 reversed

I
Cut 1 and
1 reversed

Thrift Block Symbolism:

The Calla-lily in this block was chosen because in "the language of flowers" the lily traditionally means modesty. The cabbage represents thrift and the buttercup symbolizes economy. The pineapple represents hospitality, demonstrating that in times of thrift we remain open to others' needs.

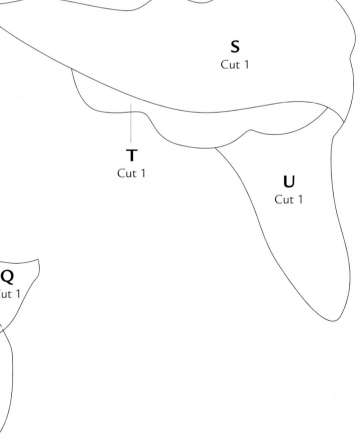

S
Cut 1

T
Cut 1

U
Cut 1

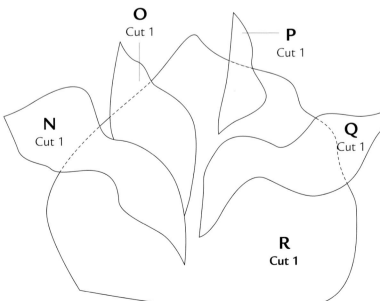

O
Cut 1

P
Cut 1

N
Cut 1

Q
Cut 1

R
Cut 1

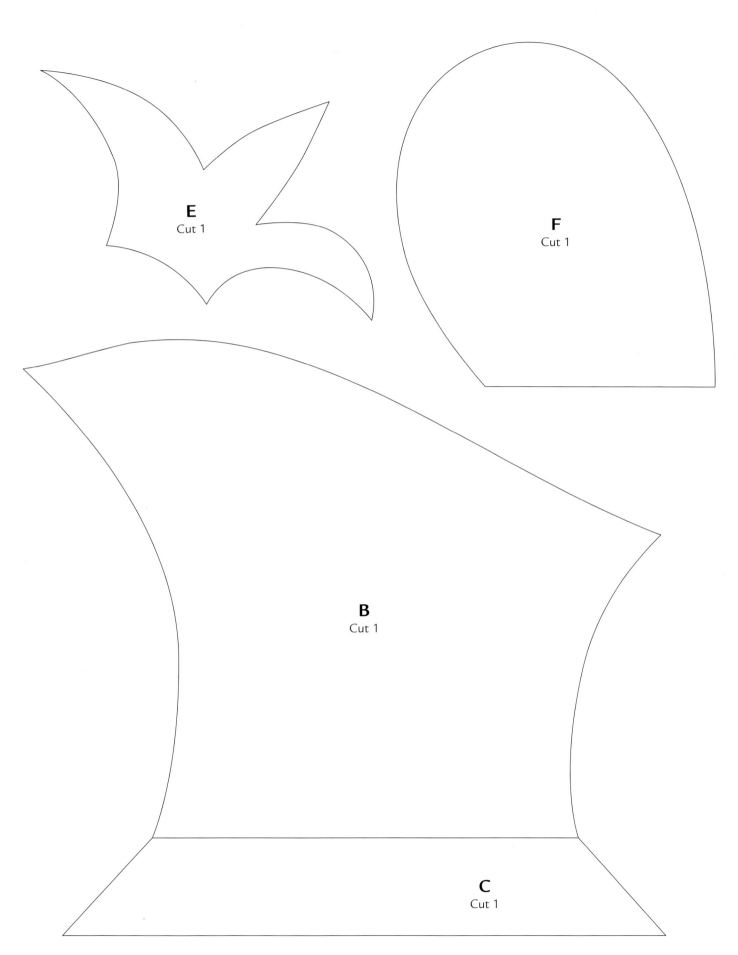

E
Cut 1

F
Cut 1

B
Cut 1

C
Cut 1

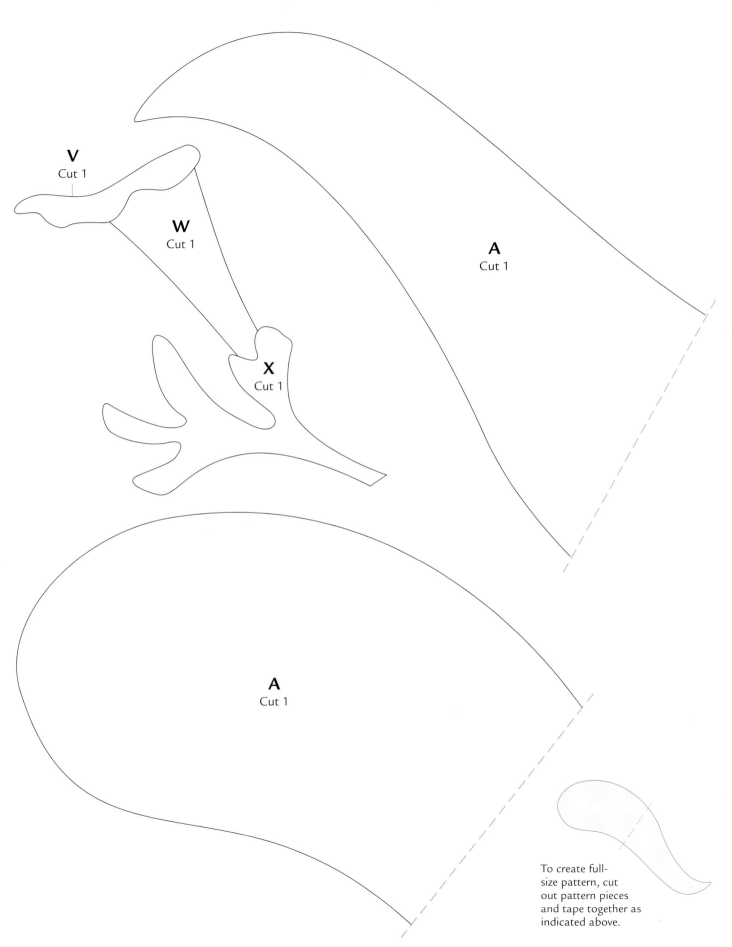

V
Cut 1

W
Cut 1

A
Cut 1

X
Cut 1

A
Cut 1

To create full-
size pattern, cut
out pattern pieces
and tape together as
indicated above.

54

M
Cut 2

L
Cut 3

J
Cut 1

K
Cut 1

D
Cut 1

G
Cut 1 and
1 reversed

Block NINE

INDUSTRY

Our inspiration:

KATE
HINKLE *(B. 1876)*

*I*T BEGAN DURING HER CHILDHOOD, the love of priceless laces and exquisite linens. Kate Hinkle would experience great pleasure in seeing them laundered properly. But as an adult, Kate despaired when she worked as a child's nurse and saw her employers discard beautiful pieces she knew were salvageable with her care. Thus came into being Kate Hinkle's French laundry, which established her as one of the earliest women entrepreneurs in Kansas City.

Her business began after her marriage ended prematurely with the death of her husband. "I've been a widow so long it's just as if I was an old maid," she would lament. Before her marriage, she had worked with the children of several wealthy families living on Quality Hill. With widowhood came the responsibility for her own livelihood. She turned to the work that came easiest to her — the laundering of laces and finely embroidered napery.

She purchased two wooden tubs, bought with her savings of $8. She then called on her former employers. From door to door, soiled bundles were placed in her handcart to be taken to her home for laundering. Many of these pieces had been passed on from generation to generation. Priceless French laces, beautiful table linens, rare old quilts, christening robes and bridal trousseaux — each piece washed and ironed by hand.

She would say that each piece had its own unique laundry problem. Previously, many owners of fine linens sent them East for laundering, so it was essential that Hinkle convince her clients that she had equal skills.

The quality of her work led to a steady increase in business, making it necessary to leave her home for larger quarters and to hire more helpers. She decided to have a building constructed to the particular needs of her business, so the operation moved into a new building at 3121 Gillham Road. Thirty women were employed to hand wash and iron. Two delivery trucks delivered the finished linens.

Hinkle exemplified the young entrepreneur, walking a long and successful road that started with two wooden tubs bought in 1908 and ended with her death in 1931, at her home above the laundry. She was 55 years old.

Pattern represents block at 39%.

Industry Block Symbolism:

The clover flower was chosen to represent industry. Thyme leaves twist with the clover stems. Thyme represents activity and strength. The two twine together symbolizing the industry our country depends upon.

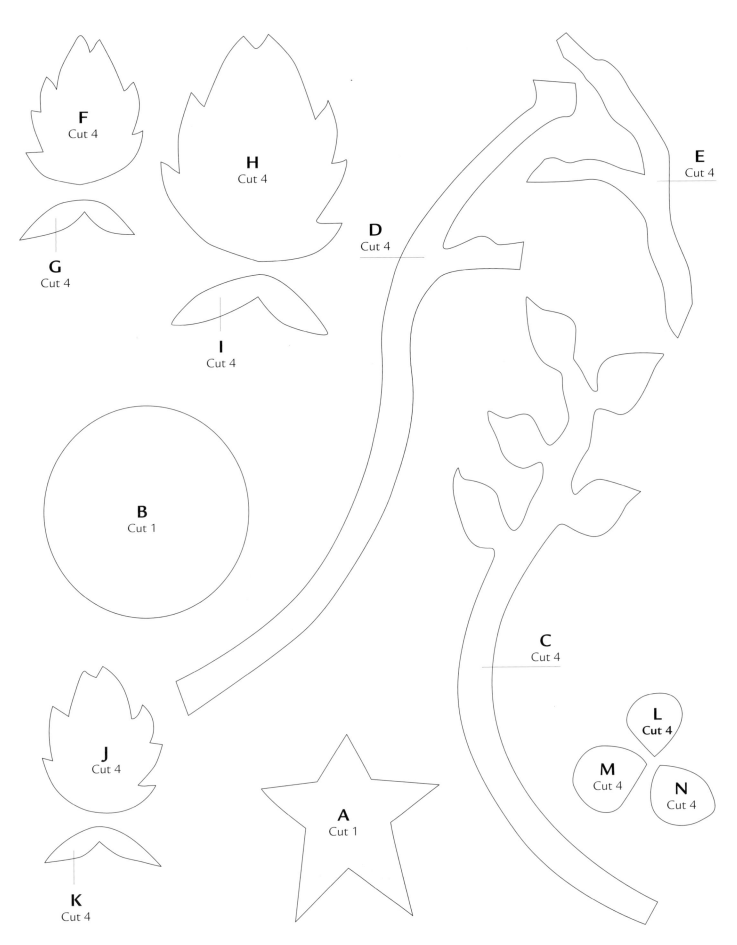

F
Cut 4

H
Cut 4

E
Cut 4

D
Cut 4

G
Cut 4

I
Cut 4

B
Cut 1

C
Cut 4

J
Cut 4

L
Cut 4

M
Cut 4

N
Cut 4

K
Cut 4

A
Cut 1

Block TEN

Our inspiration:

NELL SNEAD *(1885-1978)*

*T*HOSE WHO WERE CLOSE FRIENDS and business associates would describe Nell Snead as a character.

She was born in 1885 in Oakdale, Neb., and taught high school English in her hometown after completing her college degree. While vacationing, she stopped in Kansas City where she was taken by what she described later as a "whim." She applied for a job with The Star. Much to her surprise she was hired. This "whim" resulted in a career with the paper that lasted more than 40 years as the fashion editor and women's page editor.

Her first assignment was on the city desk, but she soon was given the women's page. She accepted on the condition that she be sent to New York City to study current fashions. The request was granted. Snead had snagged a dream job. During her career she covered numerous Paris fashion openings, the coronation of King George VI, the wedding of the Duke and Duchess of Windsor, the Suez Conference and the coronation of Queen Elizabeth II.

But she also had a knack for the homespun. As features editor, she introduced the series of Star quilt patterns that would please readers for generations across the Midwest.

When she began with the paper there were only four women employees. Over the years, she encouraged more to be hired. With her teaching instincts, she trained on her desk 16 women who were identified as "Nell's chicks."

She loved excitement and an occasional brush with danger. In 1957, Snead was a passenger on a plane en route from Paris to London when it crashed near Boulogne, France. "We were being served an excellent French meal when the plane fell," she later recalled. Fortunately, she survived. To leave no doubt in the minds of her rescuers, she yelled, "I'm not dead!" as she was hauled from the wreckage.

Snead died in 1978 at the age of 92. To the end she lived her creed, "A woman without fashion sense is like an egg without salt."

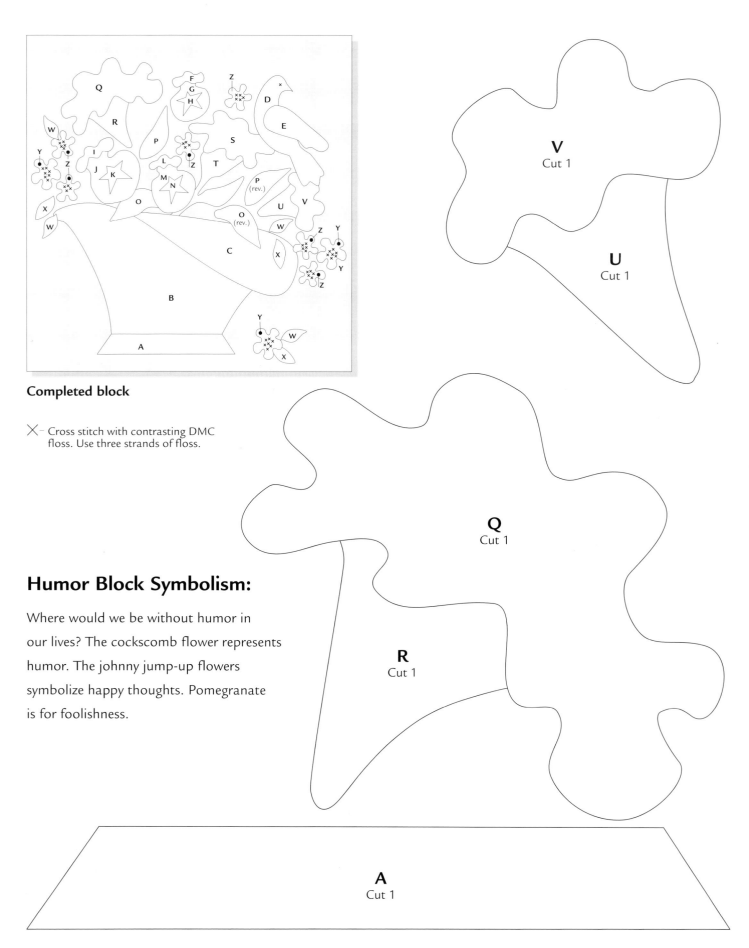

Completed block

X – Cross stitch with contrasting DMC floss. Use three strands of floss.

Humor Block Symbolism:

Where would we be without humor in our lives? The cockscomb flower represents humor. The johnny jump-up flowers symbolize happy thoughts. Pomegranate is for foolishness.

V
Cut 1

U
Cut 1

Q
Cut 1

R
Cut 1

A
Cut 1

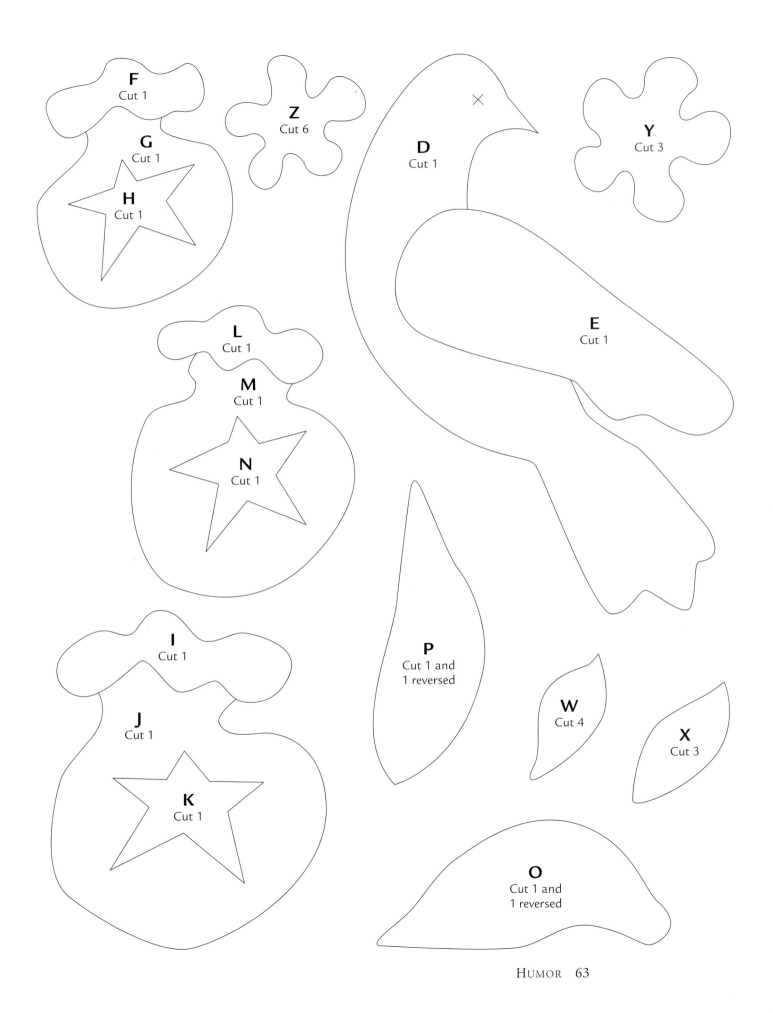

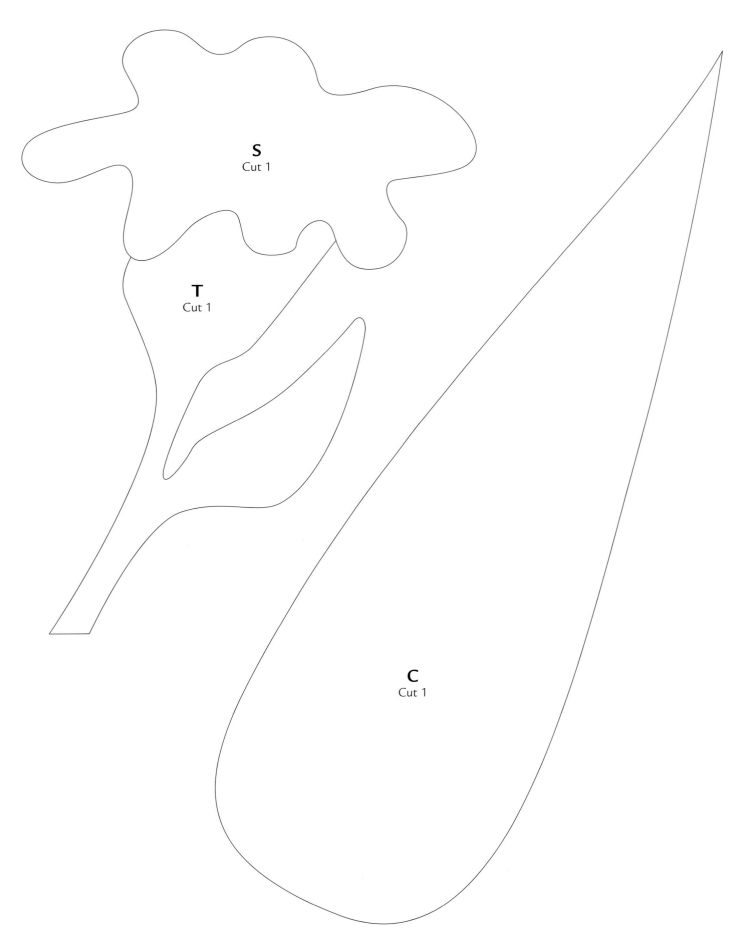

S
Cut 1

T
Cut 1

C
Cut 1

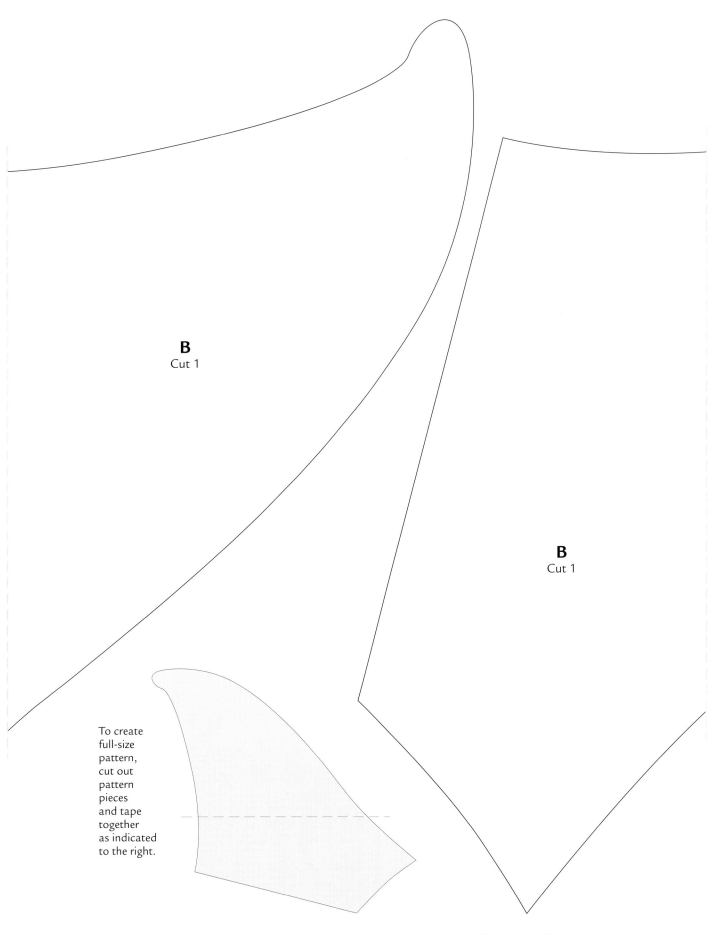

B
Cut 1

B
Cut 1

To create
full-size
pattern,
cut out
pattern
pieces
and tape
together
as indicated
to the right.

Block ELEVEN

PERSEVERANCE

Our inspiration:

LOUISA POTEET JOHNSTON *(1890-1979)*

*I*T IS HARD TO CONCEIVE that this small, wiry woman led for decades a one-woman battle to preserve for posterity one of the Kansas City area's most significant landmarks. Fearlessly taking on potential developers and indifferent government representatives, Louisa P. Johnston out-talked, out-maneuvered and seemingly out-smarted all of those who wished to demolish the landmark — the home of Alexander Majors, Johnston's great-grandfather.

Majors, Kansas City's first millionaire, was a partner in the freighting firm of Russell, Majors and Waddell Transportation Co. At one time the firm's assets included 3,500 wagons, 40,000 oxen, 1,000 mules and 4,000 men. The firm's land, over 320 acres, was used for grazing the oxen and coordinating the freight trains as they moved people and supplies to the West. Majors was also well known as a co-founder of the Pony Express. Majors' house was constructed in 1856 at 8145 State Line Road in Kansas City.

Born in 1890 the daughter of William Barnett Johnston and Susan A. Simpson, Louisa remembered little of her great-grandfather because he died when she was 10 years old. She, however, realized his importance in the settling of the West, and the house was tangible evidence of his activities. After having several owners, the house was acquired by Louisa in 1931. The house had been abused by the previous owners and by vandals. She managed on a small teacher's salary to improve, repair and restore the house. Sections of the roof, window pane by window pane, were repaired or replaced as funds were available. She admitted being too busy to consider marriage and that she limited herself to only four hours of sleep each night. The other hours were dedicated to composing letters to anyone she felt would lend support.

Initially Louisa wanted not only the house to be a part of a memorial to her great-grandfather, but also a 40-acre park eventually containing out buildings. But the area adjacent to her property was ripe for commercial development, forcing her in 1968 to settle for a 22-acre park. The house now sits on 1.1 acres.

In 1970, the Majors house was accorded the honor of being listed on the National Register of Historic Places. That it is standing today with such a designation is due solely to the perseverance, love and personal sacrifice of this woman.

Pattern represents block at 39%.

Perseverance Block Symbolism:

The ivy and blue bell flower represent constancy. The pine is a symbol of endurance with its evergreen needles. The wreath's circle reminds us that the spirit of persistence against difficulty is never ending.

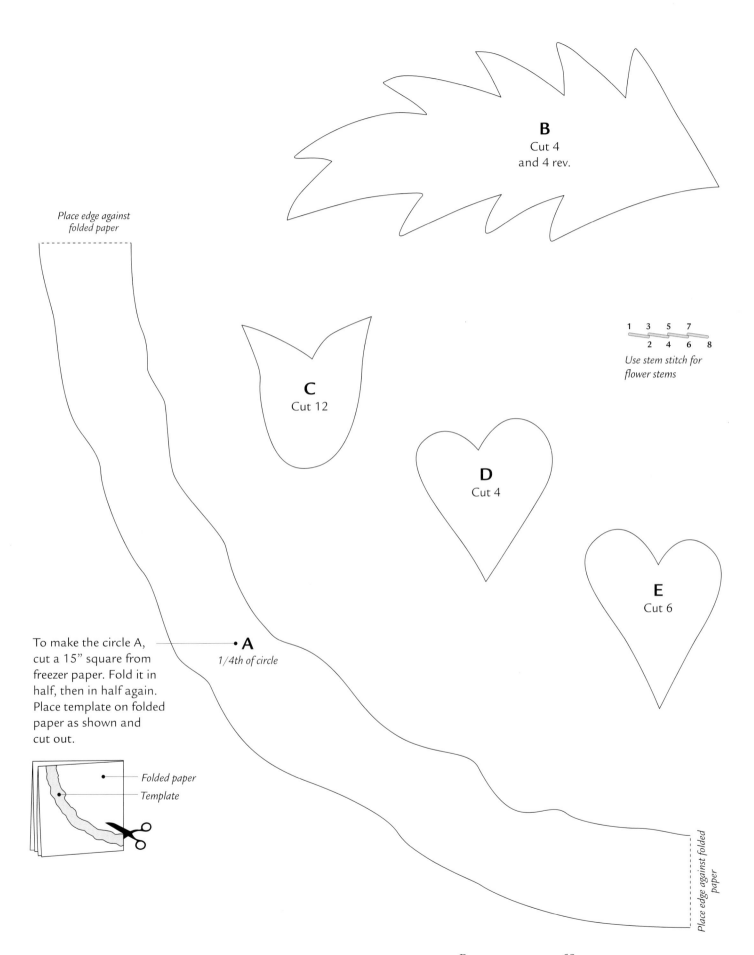

B
Cut 4
and 4 rev.

*Place edge against
folded paper*

1 3 5 7
2 4 6 8

*Use stem stitch for
flower stems*

C
Cut 12

D
Cut 4

E
Cut 6

To make the circle A,
cut a 15" square from
freezer paper. Fold it in
half, then in half again.
Place template on folded
paper as shown and
cut out.

• **A**

1/4th of circle

Folded paper
Template

*Place edge against folded
paper*

Block TWELVE

Charity

Our inspiration:

DELLA COCHRANE
LAMB *(d. 1951)*

*I*T IS DIFFICULT TO SINGLE OUT a community servant in Kansas City whose whole life of selfless service to the needy was any greater than that of Della Cochrane Lamb. For more than 50 years, guided by her deep religious beliefs, she ministered to those whose circumstances made life an overwhelming challenge.

As a child, Della Cochrane moved with her family from Bloomington, Ill., to a home at 1807 East Seventh St. in Kansas City where her father, Luman H. Cochrane, operated a fruit produce business at the City Market. As a young teenager she observed first hand the influx of immigrants moving into the area and the pressures in their lives.

Cochrane was aghast to learn of the many instances when older children had to stay at home to care for babies so mothers could go to work. Knowing the importance of an education, she became active in the Melrose Methodist Church located near her home. In 1897, the women of the church opened a day nursery. Cochrane became one of the first volunteers.

Cochrane's personal life changed with her marriage to Col. Fred A. Lamb, a former Kansas City police commissioner who shared her interest in working with children and the underprivileged. Tragically, in 1937, he lost his life in an automobile accident. Life dealt more blows with the loss of her two children, both of whom died following brief illnesses.

With the loss of her immediate family, she found solace in her religion and in continued service in the North End community. In 1903 the City Mission, in conjunction with the Methodist Church, built the Institutional Church and Neighborhood House located at 702 Admiral Boulevard. The house contained a gymnasium, one of the first public ones in the city. Also, a day nursery, a sewing school, a free medical clinic, a kindergarten, a pure milk department, a summer ice program, and dining and play rooms. These services were revolutionary in that they went outside the usual religious practices of the church.

It's no surprise that Lamb became recognized nationally among the Methodists for her community work.

Completed block

Charity Block Symbolism:

Even with our nation's abundance, we still help those in need. Charity is symbolized by the tulip. Holly represents goodwill. The small forget-me-not flower reminds us to remember those in need. The orange represents generosity. All are offered together in a basket.

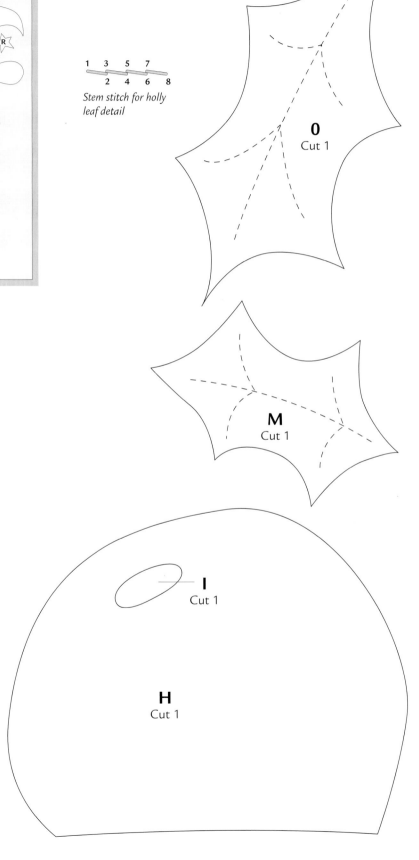

1	3	5	7
2	4	6	8

Stem stitch for holly leaf detail

O
Cut 1

M
Cut 1

I
Cut 1

H
Cut 1

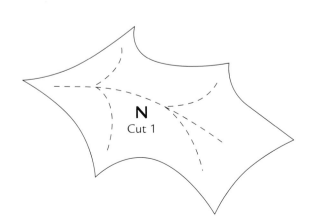

N
Cut 1

72

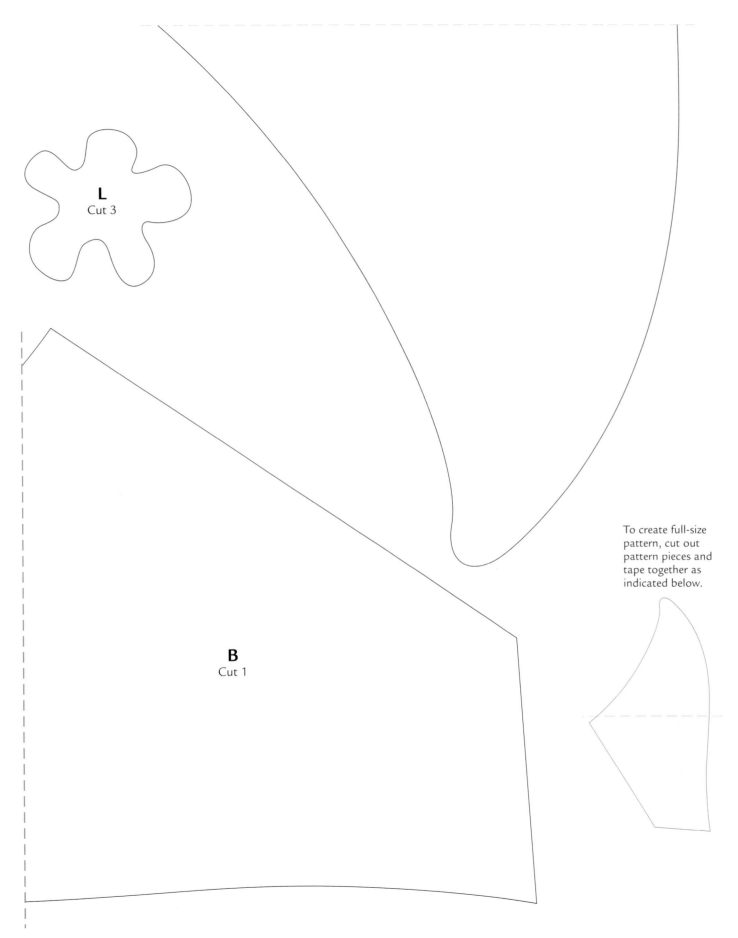

L
Cut 3

B
Cut 1

To create full-size
pattern, cut out
pattern pieces and
tape together as
indicated below.

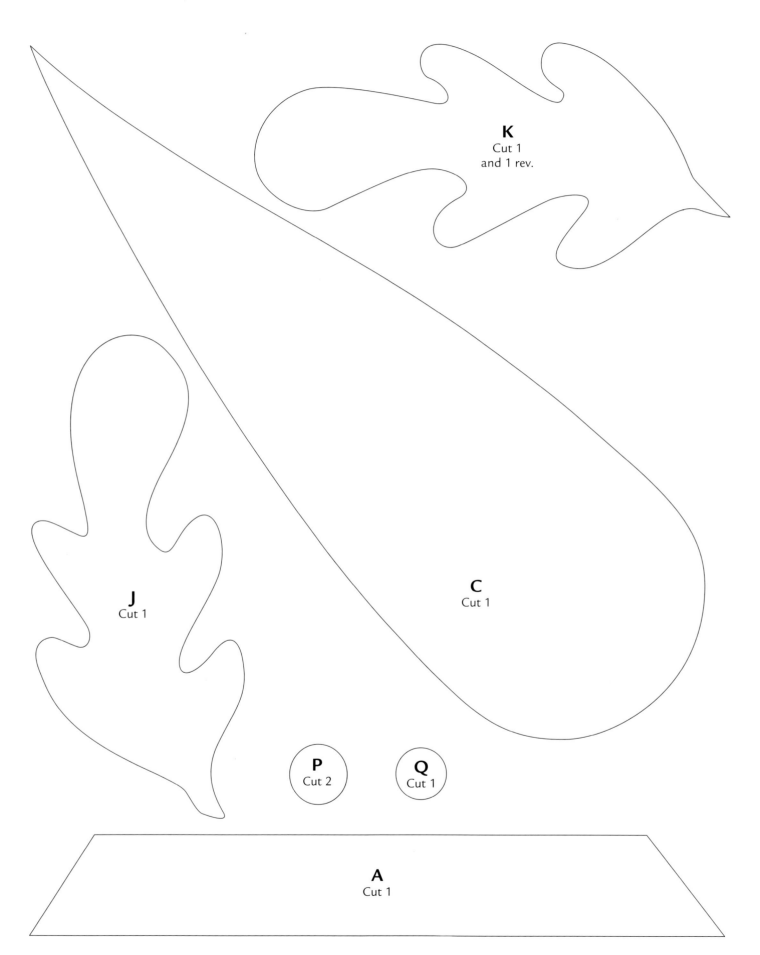

K
Cut 1
and 1 rev.

J
Cut 1

C
Cut 1

P
Cut 2

Q
Cut 1

A
Cut 1

74

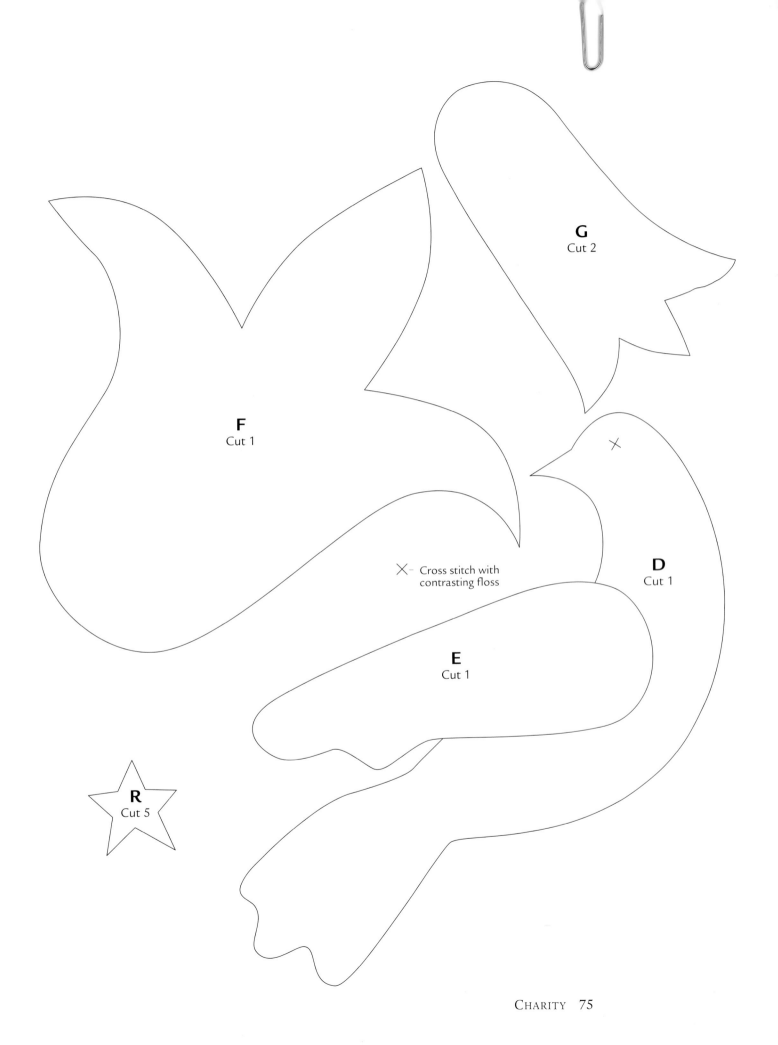

G
Cut 2

F
Cut 1

✕ - Cross stitch with
contrasting floss

D
Cut 1

E
Cut 1

R
Cut 5

Assembling & Finishing

Barb's Quilt

Begin with the pallet of fabrics suggested in the supply list. Add scraps of other prints to expand your fabric choice for each block. Barb used the "wrong" side of the ticking fabric.

BARB'S BLOCK SUPPLY LIST

4-1/4 yds. ticking for background

1/2 yd. each of 5 green fabrics for leaves and stems

1/2 yd. each of 3 red prints for flowers

1/2 yd. red floral print for the flowers, house and ribbon

1/2 yd. each of 2 tan basket prints

Fat quarter of red and tan check for the baskets

Fat quarter of tan stripe for the ribbon

Fat quarter each of 5 blue prints for the flowers, stars, ribbon detail and birds

---

BARB'S BORDER AND SASHING SUPPLY LIST

1 yd. light blue print

2 yds. medium blue

1/2 yd. dark blue

2-1/2 yds. ticking

1/2 yd. green

1/2 yd. red

Quilt Top Construction

- Cut 17 sashing strips 3-1/2" x 18-1/2" from the medium blue solid fabric.

- Cut 6 squares 3-1/2" x 3-1/2" from the dark blue print.

- Cut 68 squares 2" x 2" from the dark blue print.

- One 2" square will be sewn to each corner of the 17 sashing strips.

- Before sewing, fold the 2" squares in half on the diagonal and finger-press the fold. This fold line will be the seam line.

- Align the 2" square, right sides together, with one corner of the sashing as shown in the diagram. Sew along the seam line and trim away excess fabric. Press open. Repeat for the 3 remaining corners.

Fig. 1

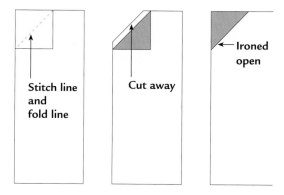

Stitch line and fold line

Cut away

← Ironed open

- Refer to Figure 1 and sew all sashing strips.

- Refer to Figure 2 and sew the quilt top together.

Triangle Border

- Cut 53 squares 4-1/4" x 4-1/4" from the light blue print. Cut in half on the diagonal twice resulting in 212 triangles.

- Cut 55 squares 4-1/4" x 4-1/4" from the medium blue solid. Cut in half on the diagonal twice resulting in 220 triangles.

- Cut 2 squares 3-7/8" x 3-7/8" from the light blue print. Cut each square in half once on the diagonal resulting in 2 triangles each. Set these aside. They are the corner triangles.

Fig. 2

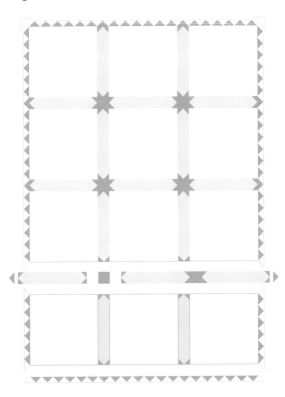

- Sew 2 strips each of 27 medium blue triangles and 26 light blue triangles. Sew one strip to each side of the quilt.

- Sew 2 strips each of 20 medium blue triangles and 19 light blue triangles. Sew one strip to the top and one to the bottom of the quilt.

- Fold the corner triangles in half to find the center. Align and sew one corner triangle to each corner of the quilt top.

BARB'S BORDER

You will need the templates from the following blocks.

1. Opportunity – flying bird
2. Humor – sitting bird
3. Humor – leaf
4. Patriotism – flower– Lily
5. Community – heart and banner

Appliqué Border

- Cut 2 borders 9-1/2" x 84-1/2" from the ticking. Sew one to each side of the quilt.

- Cut 2 borders 9-1/2" x 63-1/2" from the ticking fabric. Sew one to the top and one to the bottom of the quilt.

- Cut 1" bias strips from green fabric for the 1/2" bias vine.

- Cut appliqué shapes needed for the border. Refer to the picture for placement.

- Appliqué the shapes in place.

Fig. 3

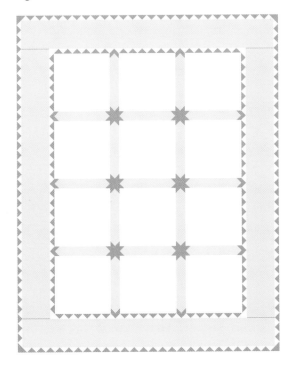

Barb's Final Triangle Border:

- Cut 2 squares 3-7/8" x 3-7/8" from the medium blue solid. Cut each square in half once on the diagonal resulting in 2 triangles each. Set these aside. They are the corner triangles.

- Sew 2 strips each of 34 light blue triangles and 33 medium blue triangles. Sew one strip to each side of the quilt.

- Sew 2 strips each of 27 light blue triangles and 26 medium blue triangles. Sew one strip to the top and one to the bottom of the quilt.

- Fold the corner triangles in half to find the center. Align and sew one corner triangle to each corner of the quilt top.

Alma's Quilt

Begin with the pallet of fabrics suggested in the supply list. Add scraps of other prints to expand your fabric choice for each block.

Quilt Construction

All measurements include a 1/4" seam allowance unless otherwise noted.

Diamond Sashing

- Cut 17 sashing strips 3-1/2" x 18-1/2" from the green print.

- Use freezer paper to make template of the appliqué diamond shape.

- Cut 17 diamonds from light tan floral print.

- Center the diamonds on the sashing strips and appliqué in place.

- Cut 6 squares 3-1/2" x 3-1/2" from the green check. These are the corner-stones between the sashing strips.

- Refer to picture and sew the blocks and sashing together to form the quilt top.

- Cut 2 strips 2" x 81-1/2" from the green print. Sew one to each side of the quilt.

- Cut 2 strips 2" x 63-1/2" from the green print. Sew one to the top and one to the bottom of the quilt.

ALMA'S QUILT BLOCK SUPPLY LIST

2-1/8 yds each of 2 light background fabrics

1/2 yd. each of 6 green fabrics for leaves and stems

1/2 yd. pink floral for flowers

Fat quarter each of 6 red-pink prints for the flowers

Fat quarter each of 2 eggplant fabrics for the birds

Fat quarter each of 7 blue fabrics for the baskets

Scraps of light blue prints for stars and flowers

Scraps of 2 orange prints

Scraps of cream prints for eagle and flag

DMC floss in green, cream and golden brown for stem stitching

---

ALMA'S BORDER AND SASHING SUPPLY LIST

1-1/2 yd. large scale tan floral for diamonds in sashing and border rectangles

2 yds. green floral for sashing, first border and binding

1/3 yd. each of 2 light prints for the border rectangle

1/4 yd. each of 6 green fabrics for the border

Diamond Template
for Sashing in
Alma's Quilt

To make diamond template, cut piece of freezer paper 3 1/2" x 18 1/2". Fold freezer paper in half. Align template fold with the fold of freezer paper. Cut template out.

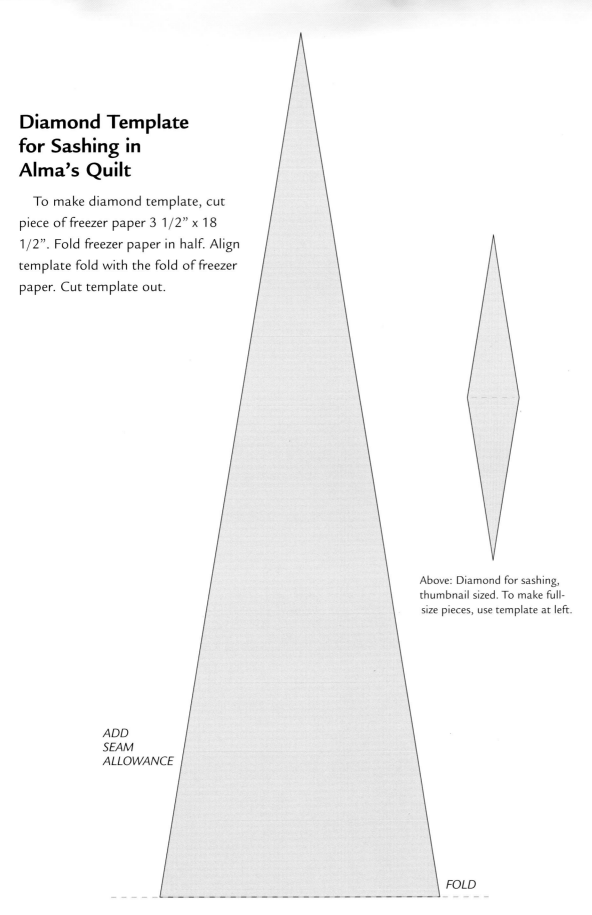

*ADD
SEAM
ALLOWANCE*

FOLD

Above: Diamond for sashing, thumbnail sized. To make full-size pieces, use template at left.

Pieced Border Instructions

- Cut 2-5/8" strips of green prints 45" wide. You will need 2 strips each of 10 prints.

- Cut (a thread under) 4-3/4" strips of light tan prints, 45" wide. You will need 1 strip each of 5 tan prints.

- Sew 4 units as illustrated in Figure 4.

Fig. 4

← 2 5/8" → ← 4 3/4" → ← 2 5/8" →

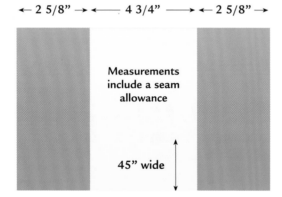

Measurements include a seam allowance

45" wide

- Press the seam allowance toward the dark green strip.

- Cut the sewn piece into 2-5/8" units as illustrated.

Fig. 5

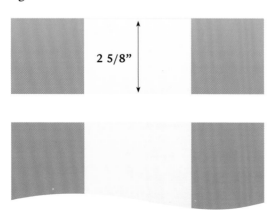

2 5/8"

Fig. 6

Seam allowance pressed to dark side

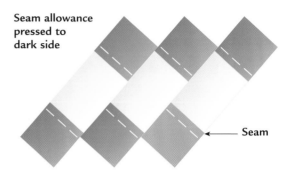

← Seam

- Sew the units together as illustrated in Figure 6. Align the second unit with the outside edge of the seam allowance of the first unit. Follow the illustration carefully when sewing the units together. When sewn, the units are directional and are only correct if sewn as illustrated.

Fig. 7

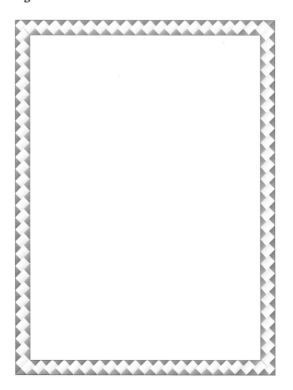

- Sew 2 strips of 27 units each for the two side borders, left and right. Refer to Figure 8 and trim the strips with a rotary cutter leaving a 1/4" seam allowance. (The triangles stretched a small amount after cutting. My border used 2 strips of 26 units each.) Sew one strip to each side of the quilt.

- Sew 2 strips of 21 units each for the top and bottom border. Refer to Figure 8 and trim the strips with a rotary cutter leaving a 1/4" seam allowance. (My border used 2 strips of 20 units each.)

Fig. 8

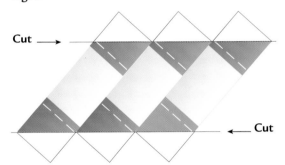

Cut →

← Cut

- Refer to the "Corner A and B" diagram Figure 9. Finish both "Corner B" sides by sewing the seams together.

Fig. 9

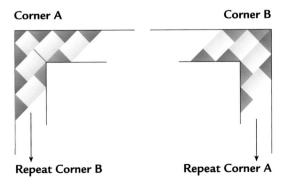

Corner A

Corner B

Repeat Corner B

Repeat Corner A

For Corner A

- Remove a triangle from one side of two units. Sew the tan rectangles together forming a strip.

- Center and sew a unit to the top of the strip.

- Cut a 4" x 4" square from a green print. Cut in half once on the diagonal.

- Refer to Figure 10 and fold the resulting triangle in half finding the center. Align the center of the triangle to the "Corner A" unit and sew.

- Sew the "Corner A" unit to the quilt top.

- Repeat for the remaining "Corner A."

Fig. 10

Corner A

Sewing Diagram Corner A

Quilt Top

LIBERTY HOOKED RUG

DESIGN BY BARB ADAMS
HOOKED BY MINERVA CABANAS
COLOR ASSISTANCE BY MARILYN SCHMIDT

Design by Barb Adams

Hooked by Minerva Cabanas

Color Assistance by
Marilyn Schmidt

*Remember to add your own initials to your rug
instead of ours! Any of the blocks' designs from
our quilt could be adapted for a hooked rug. If
you do not add the words, a circle with a 20"
diameter would work well for any of the blocks.*

Basic Instructions

- Cut your monk's cloth to 36" x 36".

  Follow a thread when possible to insure
  that the top and bottom lines are
  straight.

- Sew around the edge of the monk's
  cloth to prevent fraying with the zig-zag
  stitch on your sewing machine.

- Draw a 26" diameter circle using a string
  compass.

  Tie a fixed loop big enough for your
  marker to easily slip into, on one end of
  an 18" string. Tie another fixed loop on
  the other end of the string, just big
  enough to slip over a pin. The distance
  between the marker and pin should be
  13". Place the pin into the center of the
  monk's cloth and draw a circle around
  the center with the marker.

- Trace the "Liberty Block" design to Red
  Dot Tracer or silk organdy with black
  permanent marker.

- Center and add the word "Liberty" to
  the top of the design. Transfer the
  design to your Monk's cloth, centering
  the design inside the drawn border.

- Wash and dry your wool or use overdyed wool to prevent fraying of the
  wool.

- Use a #6 cut on your wool strips.

- Hook the shapes first. Refer to the picture for color selection.

SUPPLY LIST

Overdyed Wool:

1 yard antique black—
background

18" x 30" red overdyed
wool— letters, heart, flag

18" x 8" brown wool-eagle
wing outline

18" x 16" brown check
wool— lower wing

18" x 7" darker brown check
wool— upper wing

18" x 4" dark brown wool—
eagle chest

18" x 8" green check wool—
leaf shading

18" x 8" green tweed
wool— leaves

18" x 8" light green
wool— leaves

18" x 4" gold wool— stars,
beak, feet and eye detail

18" x 5" gray check
wool— eagle head and tail

18" x 4" blue overdyed
wool— flag

....

Permanent black marker

Red Dot Tracer or silk
organdy

1 yd. Monk's cloth

3 yd. black twill tape

Wool yard to bind rug

Rug frame

Hook

- Outline the shape areas first and then fill in with wool.

- Hook the background last.

Finishing Techniques

- Dampen a towel and place it on your finished rug. Iron with a medium steam iron through the towel.

- Bind the edges with black wool yarn.

- Trim the edges to 1/2" and sew twill tape over the raw edges.

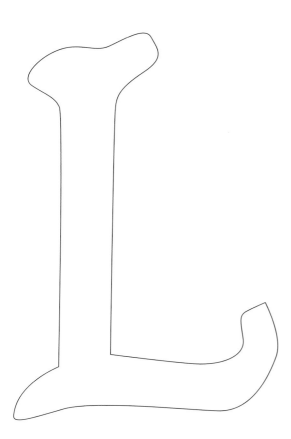

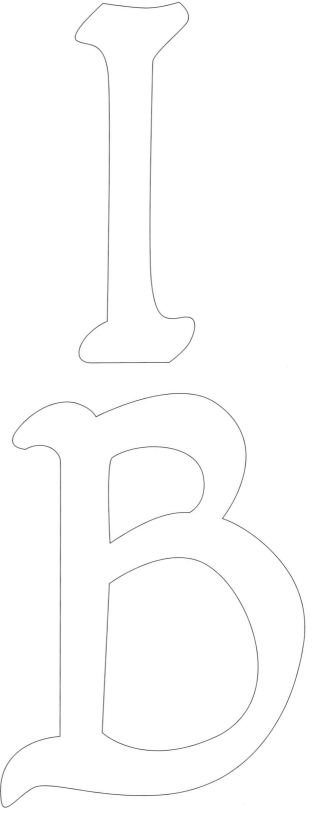

Rug is 26 inches in diameter. Shown at 32%. Grid squares egual 1 inch.

D
Draw 1
and 1 rev.

F
Draw 1
and 1 rev.

C

H

UNITED WE STAND SAMPLER

DESIGN BY BARB ADAMS
CROSS-STITCH BY JOY HAYWARD

The sampler is based on our quilt block "community." The house is surrounded by pholx flowers. In the language of flowers, the phlox flower means "our souls are united." Barb and I thought this was a nice symbol for our community.

Supply List

Linen- 22" x 13" of 30 ct linen

Over-dyed Sampler Threads by Gentle Arts

DMC floss

Tapestry Needle

Sampler Size

240H x 103W

Model

Stitched on 30 ct. linen

Linen Color

Sheep-straw linen by R & R Reproductions

Basic Instructions

- Fold to find the center of the linen. Begin stitching the center of the design at this center fold.
- Cross stitch the design using two strands of floss over two linen threads.

Symbol Guide

● Mulberry

S Nutmeg

8 Rasberry Parfait

/ Flax

◣ Old Blue Paint

× Tarnished Gold

◑ Maple Syrup

✖ Barn Gray

□ DMC 3011

— Rhubarb

• Brandy

⧓ Cinnamon

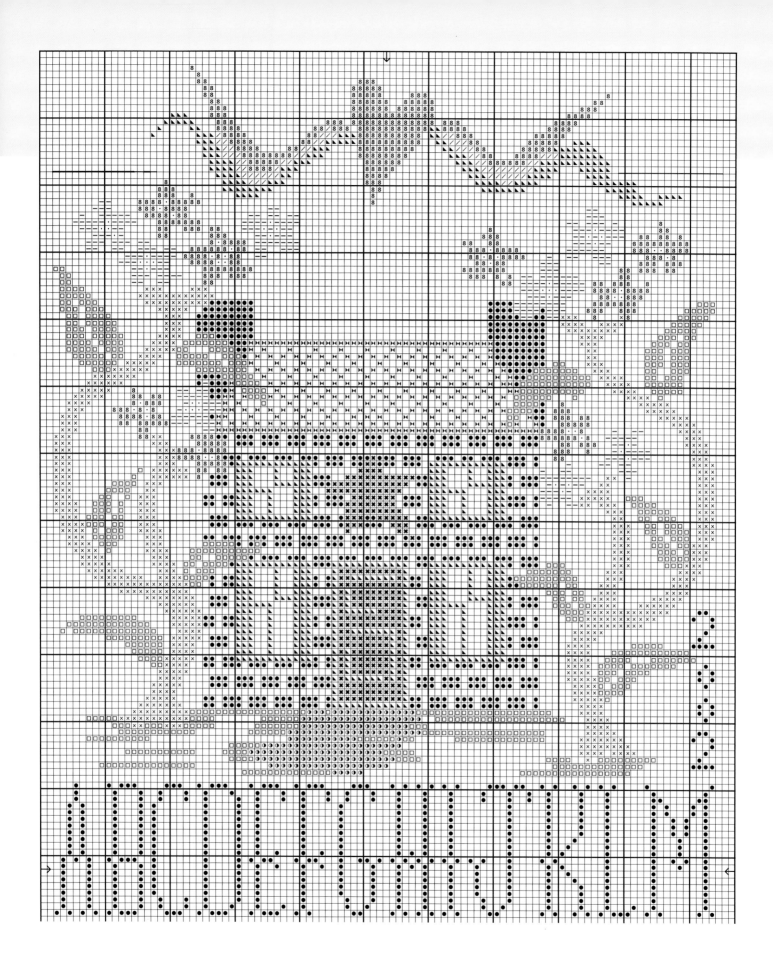

Stitch Guide – Top

Stitch Guide – Bottom

UNITED WE STAND CROSS-STITCH PILLOW

DESIGN BY BARB ADAMS
CROSS-STITCH BY SYLVIA WEBB
PILLOW CONSTRUCTION BY LEONA ADAMS

It's amazing how a small color change can transform the appearance of a cross-stitch design! This pillow uses the bottom section of the UNITED WE STAND sampler pattern. The color "Raspberry Parfait" by Gentle Arts gives sparkle to the ribbon and heart.

Basic Instructions

All measurements include a 1/4" seam allowance.

- Use the bottom section of the graph for UNITED WE STAND SAMPLER.

- Stitch all of the design except where the symbol / is shown. Leave the area where the symbol / is shown empty.

- Fold to find the center of the linen. Begin stitching the center of the design at this center fold.

- Cross-stitch the design using 2 strands of Raspberry Parfait floss over 2 linen threads.

- Cut the pillow backing 6-1/2" X 11-1/4" from the ticking fabric and set aside.

Pillow finishing:

- Cut 6" wide bias strips from the ticking fabric and sew them together for the ruffle. You will need about 75" in length.

- Fold the ruffle in half lengthwise, wrong sides together and press.

- Gather the ruffle. With right sides together, pin the ruffle to the pillow top.

While pinning, ease the gathered ruffle evenly around the pillow top.

- Sew ruffle to the pillow top.

- Sew the pillow front to the pillow back right sides together. Use a 1/4" seam allowance. Leave a 5" opening on the bottom seam for turning.

- Turn and stuff with poly-fil. Blind stitch the opening closed.

CELEBRATION PURSE

DESIGN BY BARB ADAMS

PURSE APPLIQUÉ AND CONSTRUCTION BY LEONA ADAMS

The red bird carries his flag proudly. This purse is the right size to hold everything you need during the day.

Basic Instructions

All measurements include a 1/4" seam allowance.

- Make templates of the purse patterns. The seam allowance is included in the template we have provided. The template can be found on Pages 99 -102.

- Cut from your fabric 1 back and 1 front.

- Cut from lining one back and front.

- Cut from fabric a band 1-3/4" x 28".

- Cut from lining a band 1-3/4" x 28".

- Use freezer paper to make templates of the appliqué shapes. Freezer paper gives stability to the wool shapes when cutting them out.

- Iron the slick side of the paper to the right side of your fabric.

- Cut the fabric shapes out. Do not add a seam allowance.

- Place the shapes on the front of the purse. Refer to the picture for placement. It helps if you pencil the seam allowance on the front of the purse. This prevents placing the shapes incorrectly.

- Remove the freezer paper.

- Baste shapes into place with tacky glue.

- Appliqué shapes onto the background

wool. Use a whip-stitch or button-hole stitch, with thread that matches the appliqué. (Or, try the blind-stitch on your machine.)

- Cross-stitch eye detail on the bird with three strands of contrasting floss.

Purse Construction

- Fold the top of the purse-front and purse-back to the inside at the 2-1/4" mark to form the facing. Iron to crease.

- Unfold the top of the purse-front and back to add the interfacing.
- Align the interfacing with the bottom of the purse-front and back. Iron interfacing to the wrong side of the purse back and front.

- Refold the facings to the back of the purse-front and back, and center the velcro tabs to the right sides of the facings. Open the facings and sew the tabs in place.

- With right sides together, stitch the front-facing to the front-lining.

- Use a 1/4" seam allowance. Repeat for the back-facing and back-lining.

- Press the front-facing and lining in place and baste along the edges to secure the facing and lining to the purse-front. Repeat for the purse-back.

- Mark the middle of the fabric-band and band-lining, which was cut 1-3/4" x 28".

- With right sides together, align the middle marks of the purse-back and fabric-band. Pin in place.

- Continue to pin the band around the body of the back of the purse, easing the fabric as you go. The band will extend about 1" on either side. This extension will be used later.

- Sew the fabric-band to the purse-back.

- Match the mid-points of the band-lining and bottom of the purse-back. The band lining is sewn on the other side of the seam allowance. This sandwiches the seam allowance of the purse back between the band and the band lining.

- Sew the band lining in place on the other side of the purse back seam allowance.

- Mark and center the fabric band to the purse front. Sew the fabric band to the purse front, right sides together.

- Fold the 1" band extensions, left and right, to the inside of the purse and whip stitch in place.

- Wrap floss around the ends of the cording to prevent fraying.

- Place 1-1/2" of one end of the rope cording along the band seam allowance and secure.

- Adjust the length of cording for shoulder strap length. Cut off excess.

- Secure the other end of the cording to the seam allowance on the opposite side.

- Bring the band lining over the front seam allowance, encasing the cording ends. Blind-stitch to cover the seam allowances.

- Turn the purse right side out.

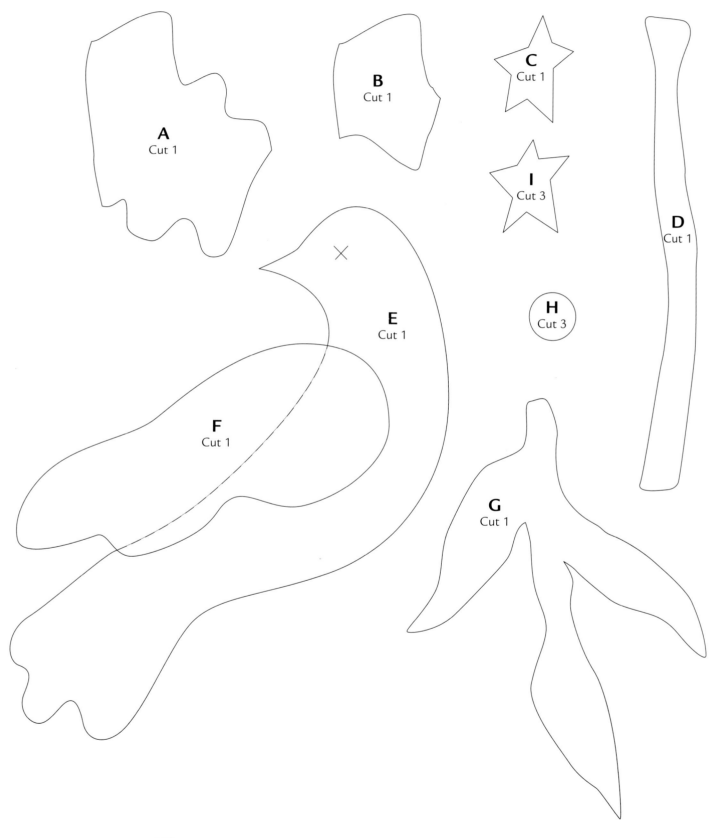

A
Cut 1

B
Cut 1

C
Cut 1

I
Cut 3

D
Cut 1

E
Cut 1

H
Cut 3

F
Cut 1

G
Cut 1

Purse Template (Top)

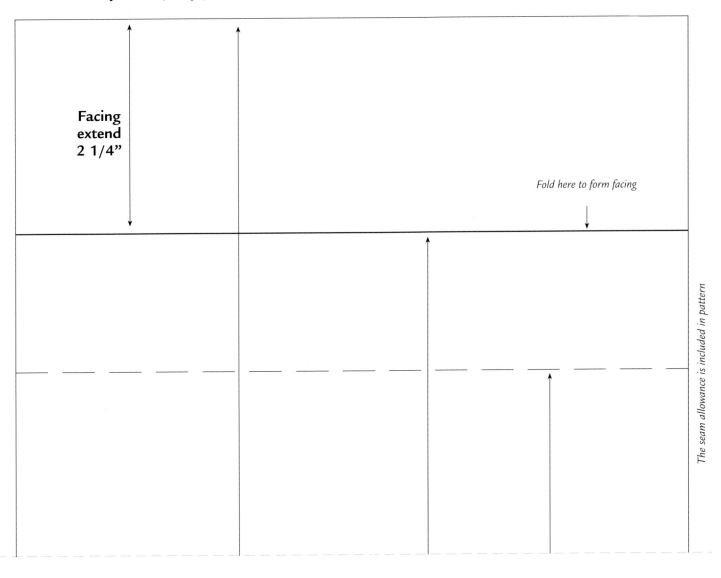

Facing extend 2 1/4"

Fold here to form facing

The seam allowance is included in pattern

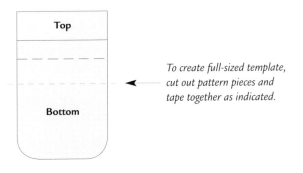

Top

Bottom

To create full-sized template, cut out pattern pieces and tape together as indicated.

Purse Template (Bottom)

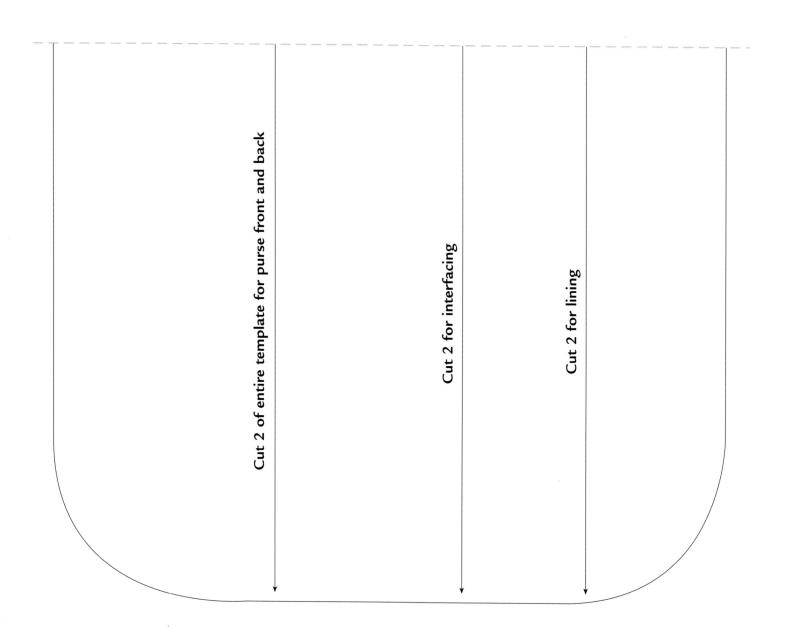

Cut 2 of entire template for purse front and back

Cut 2 for interfacing

Cut 2 for lining

CROCHET FLAG PILLOW

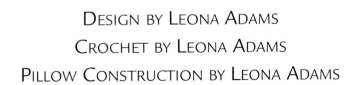

DESIGN BY LEONA ADAMS

CROCHET BY LEONA ADAMS

PILLOW CONSTRUCTION BY LEONA ADAMS

DESIGN BY LEONA ADAMS

CROCHET BY LEONA ADAMS

PILLOW CONSTRUCTION BY
LEONA ADAMS

We are fortunate to have Barb's mother, Leona! Leona's skills and understanding of the sewing process never fail to come to our rescue. Many times she has worked on some of our projects into the late hours of the night. Her pillow design is a dear addition to this book.

SUPPLY LIST

Knit Cro-Sheen- Crochet thread Art- A-65 (#10 thread):

Ecru #16

Cardinal Red #196

Dark Royal Blue #87

Steel Crochet hook #8

Tapestry needle #18

Rit dye- tan #16

1- 12 oz. bag of polyfil

Abbreviations

- *beg* – beginning
- *ch(s)* – chain, chains -yo, pull through loop on hook
- *sc* – single crochet-Insert hook in st, yo, pull through st, yo, pull through both loops on hook
- *dc* – double crochet- yo-insert hook in st, yo, pull through st, (yo, pull through 2 loops) 2 times
- *hdc* – half double crochet- Yo, insert hook in st, yo, pullthrough st, yo, pull through all 3 loops on hook.
- *sl st* – slip stitch
- *st(s)* – stitch or stitches

Crochet Instructions

Note: Three rows of dc make the large stripes. This flag is worked from the bottom to the top alternating red and ecru stripes. When adding a new color of cord hold the end of the new color along the row and cover as you dc. Ch 3 counts as dc in every row.

Begin with red thread:

- Row 1– Ch 103, Work dc in third chain from the hook and in each ch across. With the last dc in row, ch 3 and turn.
- Row 2– Dc across row for a total of 100 dc. Ch 3 and turn.
- Row 3– Repeat row 2. With last dc in row pull through 2 loops. Cut off thread leaving 3 inches. Add the ecru thread pull through 2 remaining loops. Ch 3 and turn.
- Row 4-6– Continue dc with ecru thread as in previous 3 red rows. The last dc pick up red thread, ch 3 and turn.
- Row 7-9– Repeat red stripe
- Row 10-12– Repeat ecru stripe
- Row 13-15– Repeat red stripe
- Row 16-18– Repeat ecru stripe
- Row 19– Dc in the next st and across

the remaining 58 sts with red thread. Dc in the next st, pull through 2 loops. Cut the thread leaving 3". Add the blue thread, pull through 2 remaining loops. Dc in the next 40 sts. Ch 3 and turn.

- Row 20– Dc in sts across the remaining 38 sts, holding the blue thread to the back and work each row picking it up. On the 39 st pull through 2 loops and pick up the red thread and pull through the 2 remaining loops. Dc across the 60 sts. Ch 3 and turn.

- Row 21– Dc in the next st and across the remaining 58 sts with red thread. Dc in the next st, pull through 2 loops and cut the thread leaving 3". Pick up the blue thread, pull through 2 remaining loops and dc in the next 40 sts. Ch 3 and turn.

- Row 22– Dc in sts across the remaining 38 sts. On the 39 st pull through 2 loops. Add the ecru thread, and pull through the 2 remaining loops. Dc across 60 sts. Ch 3 and turn.

- Row 23– Dc in the next st and across the remaining 58 sts with ecru thread. Dc in the next st and pull through 2 loops. Cut the thread leaving 3". Pick up the blue thread and pull through the 2 remaining loops. Dc in the next 40 sts. Ch 3 and turn.

- Row 24– Dc in the sts across the remaining 38 sts. Dc in the 39 st. Pull through 2 loops, picking up the ecru

thread. Pull through 2 remaining loops and dc across the 60 sts. Ch 3 and turn.

- Rows 25-27– Repeat rows 19-21 with red thread.

- Rows 28-30– Repeat rows 22-24 with ecru thread.

- Rows 31-33– Repeat rows 19-21 with red thread.

- At the end of row 33 cut the blue thread leaving 3".

Securing Thread Ends

Using a large eyed needle, weave the thread ends through the crochet stitches and trim.

Star Crochet Instructions

Begin with Ecru thread-

- Ch 5, sl st to form a circle.

- Row 1– Ch 3, sl into circle and make a total of 21 dc. Sl in top of beg dc.

- Row 2– Ch 3, dc into 6 sts. Ch 3, turn.

- Row 3– Dc into 4 sts. Ch 3 and turn.

- Row 4– Dc next st, taking only 2 loops off and hdc into the next sts, finishing the point. Cut the thread leaving 3". Work the loose thread into the back, tightening the point.

- Repeat the remaining 4 points to form the star.

- Shape into a star. Using ecru thread, whip-stitch the star to the blue background of the flag.

Overdye Instructions

- Mix 1/4 cup dye with 2 cups water. Wet the flag with plain water and dip the wet flag into the dye solution. The flag will appear darker in the dye solution but dries lighter. Rinse in clear water and add 2 tablespoons of salt in the rinse water. Continue to rinse until clear.

- Roll the design in paper towels to absorb excess moisture. Shape and gently stretch to dry.

Pillow Instructions

Seam allowance of 1/2" included in the measurement.

- Cut a rectangle 13" x 18" from ticking fabric.

- Fold the ticking in half, right sides together, forming a 13" x 9" rectangle. Using a 1/2" seam allowance, sew the pillow front to the pillow, back, right sides together. Leave a 5" opening on the bottom seam for turning.

- Turn and whip-stitch the flag to the pillow front.

- Stuff with poly-fil. Blind-stitch the opening closed.

PATRIOTIC BLUE WORK PILLOW

DESIGN BY BARB ADAMS
BLUE WORK BY LEONA ADAMS
PILLOW CONSTRUCTION BY LEONA ADAMS

DESIGN BY BARB ADAMS

BLUE WORK BY LEONA ADAMS

PILLOW CONSTRUCTION BY
LEONA ADAMS

*This sweet pillow will be comfortable anywhere in
your home. The patriotic block has been reduced
to nine inches. The blue jaccard is by MODA fabrics. The stars sprinkled liberally over the fabric is
the perfect backgound for this bluework.*

*As you look at the blocks in the book, remember
any of them could be reduced and substituted in
the center of this pillow.*

SUPPLY LIST

1 yd. light blue jaccard for background, ruffle and pillow backing (MODA fabrics)	Sulky Water Soluble Stabilizer
1/4 yd. slate blue jaccard	Sulky temporary fabric spray adhesive
2 skeins DMC #930	1- 10 oz. bags of Poly-fil

Basic Instructions

All measurements include a 1/4" seam
allowance.

- Cut the background block 10-1/2" X 10-1/2".

- Cut pillow backing 14-1/2" X 14-1/2" and set aside.

- Trace the design to the Sulky water soluble stabilizer.

- Spray the back of the stabilizer with Sulky temporary-fabric-spray adhesive. Center and position the stabilizer to the top of the background block.

- Stem-stitch the design with 4 strands of DMC #930 floss using a large eye embroidery needle.

- Stitch the berries with the satin-stitch.

- Cut away most of the stabilizer from the design when the stitching is completed. Remove the stabilizer from the design following the product instructions.

- Cut 2 borders 2-1/2" x 10-1/2". Sew one strip to the top of the pillow design and one to the bottom.

- Cut 2 borders 2-1/2" x 14-1/2". Sew one strip to each side of the pillow top.

- Cut 8" wide bias strips and sew them together for the ruffle. You will need about 4 yards length for the ruffle.

- Fold the ruffle in half lengthwise, wrong sides together and press.

- Gather the ruffle. With right sides together, pin the ruffle to the pillow top. While pinning, ease the gathered ruffle evenly around the pillow top.

- Sew ruffle to the pillow top.

- Sew the pillow front to the pillow back right sides together. Use a 1/4" seam allowance. Leave a 6" opening on the bottom seam for turning.

■ Turn and stuff with poly-fil. Blind stitch the opening closed.

Stem-stitch the design with 4 strands of DMC #930 floss using a large eye embroidery needle.

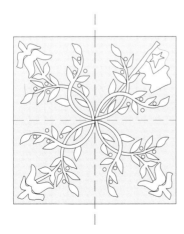

To create full-sized template, draw the pattern and tape together as indicated.

CHARITY PENNY MAT

DESIGN BY ALMA ALLEN
STITCHED BY ALMA ALLEN

DESIGN BY ALMA ALLEN

STITCHED BY ALMA ALLEN

The "Charity" block has been reduced to 11" for this penny mat. The penny mat is finished using the same technique as a pillow. The only difference is the mat does not have any stuffing.

If you would like to make this into a pillow use the same finishing instructions and add stuffing before whipping the front and back closed.

SUPPLY LIST

1/2 yd. green print for top and backing

12" square khaki green over-dyed wool— background

6" x 7" gold wool— basket

3" x 6" gold wool check— basket

3" x 5" blue wool check— bird

1-1/2" x 3" blue overdyed wool— bird's wing

Scraps of 4 green wool

overdyed and checks— leaves

Scraps of light blue wool— flowers

3" x 3" orange wool— orange

4-1/2" x 4" rose wool— tulip

Scraps of rose shades— two small tulips

Scraps of light gold— stars and initials

DMC floss to match wool colors

Basic Instructions

All measurements include a 1/4" seam allowance.

- Cut the background block 11-1/2" x 11-

1/2" from the khaki green wool fabric.

- Cut 2 squares for the mat's top and backing 14-3/4" x 14-3/4" and set aside.

- Use freezer-paper to make templates of the appliqué shapes. Freezer-paper gives stability to the wool shapes when cutting them out.

- Iron the slick side of the paper to the right side of your fabric.

- Cut the fabric shapes out. Do not add a seam allowance.

- Place the shapes on your background block. Refer to the picture for placement.

- Remove the freezer paper.

- Baste shapes into place with tacky glue.

- Appliqué the shapes to the background wool using the button-hole stitch with 2 strands of matching DMC floss.

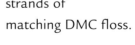

Button-hole Stitch

- Stitch detail in the leaves with the stem-stitch using 2 strands of contrasting floss.

Finishing Instructions

- Center the wool block on the right side of the 14-3/4" fabric square.

- Baste the wool block to the fabric

square with tacky glue.

- Stitch the wool block to the fabric square using the button-hole stitch and 2 strands of floss.

- Sew the mat front to the mat backing, right sides together. Use a 1/4" seam allowance. Leave a 6" opening on the bottom seam for turning.

- Turn and blind stitch the opening closed.

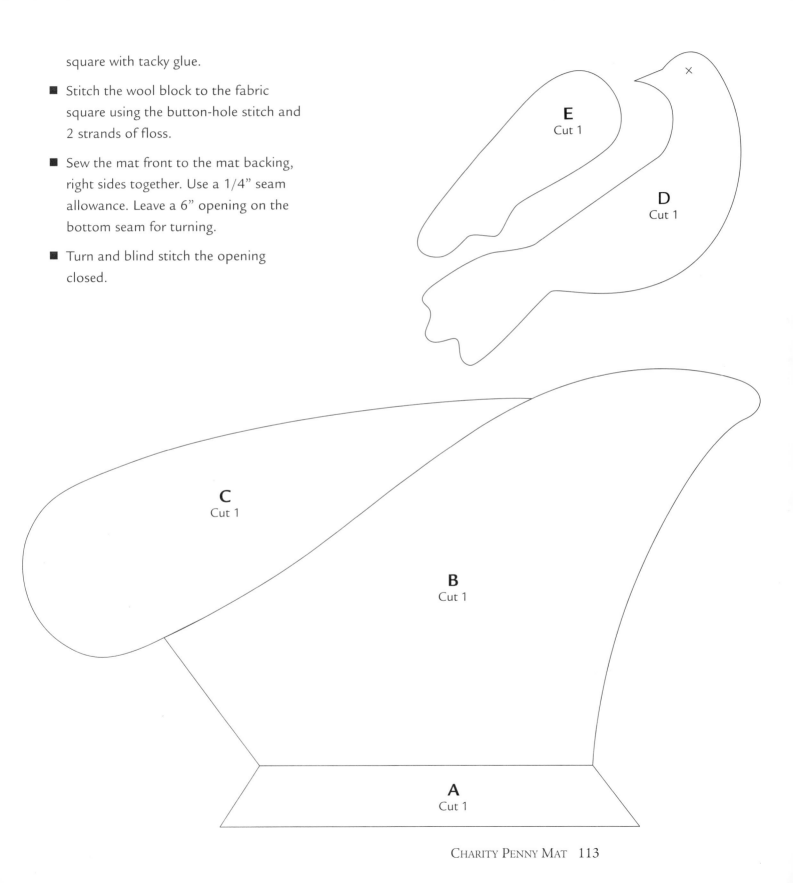

E
Cut 1

D
Cut 1

C
Cut 1

B
Cut 1

A
Cut 1

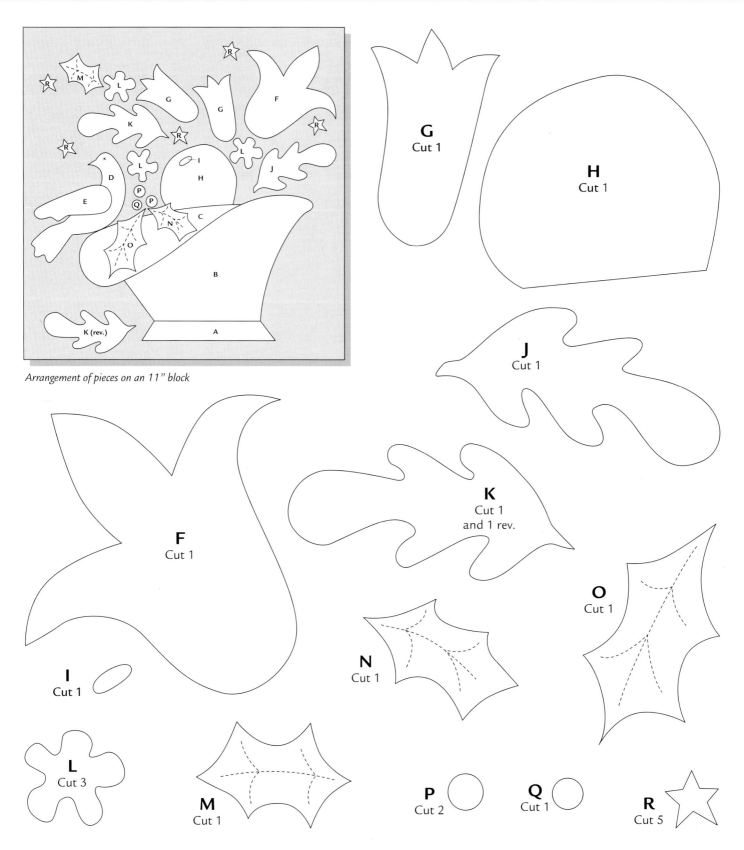

Arrangement of pieces on an 11" block

G
Cut 1

H
Cut 1

J
Cut 1

K
Cut 1
and 1 rev.

O
Cut 1

N
Cut 1

F
Cut 1

I
Cut 1

L
Cut 3

M
Cut 1

P
Cut 2

Q
Cut 1

R
Cut 5

FERN PINCUSHION

 STITCHING AND COLOR DESIGN BY KATHLEEN JOHNSON

PINCUSHION CONSTRUCTION BY LEONA ADAMS

STITCHING AND COLOR DESIGN
BY KATHLEEN JOHNSON

PINCUSHION CONSTRUCTION BY
LEONA ADAMS

Everyone should be so lucky! When Kathleen attended our class she brought us a wonderful gift. She made pincushions for Barb and me from some of our quilt designs. We were amazed to see her creations. We asked her to stitch one for our book. This small fern block was our choice.

Kathleen used the colonial knot to fill the design area. The colonial knots lay flatter and fill better than french knots. Her use of over-dyed floss gives shading and depth to the design. Kathleen uses two threads together in the larger areas and only one thread in smaller detail areas.

Basic Instructions

- Cut your background fabric 8" x 8".

- Cut a muslin square 8" x 8".

- Using a light box, center and trace the design on the right side of the background fabric.

- Place the background fabric on the top of the muslin square right side up.

- Work through both fabrics as one. The muslin gives stability.

- Place the background fabric, together with the muslin, into a small hoop.

- Begin stitching. Use one thread for the knot area in the ribbon and the stars, and two threads everywhere else. Outline a small area with knots, then fill in. Do not crowd or leave gaps for the background to show through. The size of the knots may vary. A consistent tension will develop as you work.

Finishing:

- Press face down on a towel. When using overdyed floss, take care not to get the design area wet because the overdyed floss is not color fast.

- Trim the background fabric to 5-1/2" x 5-1/2".

SUPPLY LIST

Weeks Dye Works floss:

Moss— right side of the fern wreath

Kudzu— left side of the fern wreath

Camilla— ribbon

Americana— stars

Lancaster red— knot in ribbon

. . . .

Sampler Threads by Gentle Arts:

Blue Jay— stars

Royal Purple— stars

Embroidery needle
Small hoop

8" square print cotton fabric

8" square of muslin

Wool— Use overdyed or washed and dried to prevent fraying. If you are going to wash and dry your wool, start with a larger piece because wool shrinks.

6-1/2" square of red check wool

8" square solid green wool

8" square of green check wool

Poly-fil

- Turn in a 1/4" seam allowance to the back, along each outside edge of all four sides of the background square. Press to crease.

- Cut a square of red-checked wool 6-1/2" x 6-1/2".

- Using the button-hole stitch, center and sew the background square to the red-checked wool square.

- Cut the backing wool out using the template provided. Cut 1 each from the solid green and the green check.

- Place in following order from table up: green checked backing, green solid backing, and red-checked wool with design area.

- Stitch 1/2" in from the edge of the red-checked wool to enclose the pincushion. Leave an opening of 3-1/2" along the bottom edge.

- Stuff the pincushion with poly-fil and stitch the opening closed.

Pattern for Fern Pincushion

MAKING A COLONIAL KNOT

BRING THE NEEDLE up where the knot is to be made. Hold the threaded needle in your right hand and hold the thread halfway between the fabric and the needle with your left hand. Keep the needle pointed toward the fabric and on top of the thread. Hook the sharp end of the needle back under the thread between the left hand and the fabric. Take the thread being held in the left hand and hook it over and under the sharp end of the needle. This should form a "figure eight" or Colonial Knot.

REINSERT THE NEEDLE into the fabric and tighten the "figure eight" around the needle taking out all the slack in the thread between the fabric and needle. Pull the needle through and your knot should be perfect.

Colonial Knot

Template for Backing

Cut 2

$\mathscr{S}$TAR QUILTS YEAR BY YEAR

Here is a chronological list — including repeats — of the quilt patterns and designs published by The Kansas City Star from 1928 through 2002.

If you'd like to see the patterns on the pages of the newspaper, microfilm copies of *The Star* are available at the Kansas City Public Library's Main Branch, 311 E. 12th St., Kansas City, Mo.

For an alphabetical list of the designs, see Wilene Smith's "Quilt Patterns: An Index to The Kansas City Star Patterns."

For a thumbnail sketch of each pattern, see Volume 5 of "The Ultimate Illustrated Index to The Kansas City Star Quilt Pattern Collection" by the Central Oklahoma Quilters Guild.

Months not listed here had no published quilt patterns.

INDEX OF PATTERNS

1928
- September
  Pine Tree
  Album Quilt
- October
  French Star
  Log Cabin
  Rob Peter and Pay Paul
  Cherry Basket
  Wedding Ring
- November
  Jacob's Ladder
  Greek Cross
  Sky Rocket
  Double T
- December
  Ocean Wave
  Wild Goose Chase
  Old Maid's Puzzle
  Rambler

1929
- January
  Weathervane
  Monkey Wrench
  Spider Web
  Irish Chain
- February
  Rising Sun
  Princess Feather
  Double Nine Patch
  Eight-Pointed Star
- March
  Goose in the Pond
  Dove in the Window
  Beautiful Star
  Broken Circle
  Beggar Block
- April

Cupid's Arrow Point
Noon Day Lily
Lafayette Orange Peel
Necktie
- May
  Duck and Ducklings
  House on the Hill
  Crossed Canoes
  Turkey Tracks
- June
  Ribbon Border Block
  Posey
  Bird's Nest
  Crosses and Losses
  Double Star
- July
  Jack in the Box
  Aircraft
  Springtime Blossoms
  Sunbeam
- August
  Saw-Tooth
  Cross and Crown
  Hands All 'Round
  Honey Bee
  Flower Pot
- September
  Susannah
  Goose Tracks
  Fish Block
  Wedding Ring
- October
  Swastika
  Seth Thomas Rose
  "V" Block
  Little Beech Tree
- November
  Palm Leaf
  Tulip Appliqué

Mill Wheel
Order No. 11
Old King Cole's Crown
- December
  Strawberry Block
  Old King Cole
  Little Wooden Soldier
  Road to Oklahoma
  (The "Santa's Parade Quilt" series ran in December 1929).

1930
- January
  Churn Dash
  Corn and Beans
  Rose Cross
  Milky Way
- February
  True Lovers Buggy Wheel
  Indiana Puzzle
  Blazing Star
  Aster
- March
  Sunflower
  Grape Basket
  Steps to the Altar
  Kaleidoscope
  Dutchman's Puzzle
- April
  English Flower Garden
  Single Wedding Ring
  Pin Wheels
  Cross and Crown
- May
  Missouri Puzzle
  Merry Go-Round
  Lone Star
  Missouri Star
  Sail Boat

- June
  Virginia Star
  Rail Fence
- July
  Mexican Star
  Basket of Oranges
  Rose Album
  Clay's Choice
- August
  Maple Leaf
  Sunbonnet Sue
  Compass
  Kaleidoscope
  Rainbow Tile
- September
  Goblet
  Calico Puzzle
  Broken Dishes
  Swallows in the Window
- October
  Secret Drawer
  Spider Web
  Marble Floor
  Pinwheel
  (The "Memory Bouquet Quilt" series ran in October 1930.)
- November
  Grandmother's Favorite
  Indian Emblem
  Friendship
  Puss in the Corner
  Sage-Bud
  (The "Memory Bouquet Quilt" series ran in November 1930).
- December
  Turnabout "T"
  Snow Crystals
  Sweet Gum Leaf
  Rose Dream

INDEX OF PATTERNS

INDEX OF PATTERNS

INDEX OF PATTERNS

INDEX OF PATTERNS

INDEX OF PATTERNS

INDEX OF PATTERNS